Falling in Love

Vernon W. Grant, on call as consultant to the state rehabilitation center in Tennessee, where he now resides, has recently been devoting himself largely to writing. His previous appointments include more than twenty years' service on the staffs of a state hospital and a psychiatric clinic in Ohio. Concurrently, for twelve years, he conducted a private practice in marriage counseling and psychotherapy. Dr. Grant graduated from the University of Chicago, did graduate work at Columbia, and received his doctorate from Northwestern University. He has taught at the University of Rochester and at St. Lawrence and Adelphi Universities, and is a fellow of the Society for the Scientific Study of Sex. A contributor to the Encyclopedia of Sexual Behavior, he has also published widely in leading professional journals and is the author of several books, including *The Psychology of Sexual Emotion* and *The Roots of Religious Doubt.*

Falling in Love

The Psychology
of the Romantic Emotion

Vernon W. Grant

Springer Publishing Company

NEW YORK

To my forerunners

Albert Moll
Alfred Binet
Henry T. Finck

Copyright © 1976 by Springer Publishing Company, Inc.

Springer Publishing Company, Inc.
200 Park Avenue South
New York, N.Y. 10003

76 77 78 79 80 / 10 9 8 7 6 5 4 3 2 1

Library of Congress Cataloging in Publication Data

Grant, Vernon W
   Falling in love.

   Bibliography: p.
   Includes index.
   1. Love—Psychological   aspects.   2. Sex   (Psychology)   I. Title.
[DNLM: 1. Love. 2. Sex behavior. BF575.L8 G763f]
BF575.L8G7   152.4   75-44446
ISBN 0-8261-1890-9
ISBN 0-8261-1891-7 pbk.

Printed in the United States of America

Contents

Preface

For centuries men have pondered the nature and causes of an emotion of great power which arises in certain encounters between the sexes, but differs markedly from the sexual impulse itself. The traits that arouse this "romantic" emotion are typically not those that stimulate sexual desire. It is, moreover, highly selective; one is romantically attracted only to persons with features and characteristics that seem exceptional, "different," somehow intriguing.

Compared with physical sexuality, very little research has been done on the romantic emotion, despite its importance in our society as the prelude to marriage. Sigmund Freud, recognizing the difference between the two motives, offered the theory that under certain conditions one changes into the other, but many have found his explanation unsatisfactory. Freud himself may have realized this when he once confessed that "we really know very little about love."

Some contemporaries of Freud, eminent in psychology but overshadowed by his authority, developed a different concept of the romantic emotion, emphasizing the ways in which it is wholly distinct from sexual attraction. Their views of romantic love are closer to those of poets and novelists, who throughout the ages have described and celebrated this phenomenon whose essence seems to lie in the realm of esthetics and as such has inspired creative works in all fields of art. For this reason we have included in our discussion a number of illustrations from literary sources as well as case studies of a variety of love experiences.

The book offers evidence and support, then, for a non-Freudian view of "falling in love." In important respects it is a simpler and more convincing account of attraction than that of Freud. We also discuss the specific traits to which different individuals respond and which cause them to develop emotional fixations.

Many young people may find this book of particular interest because, in dealing with a topic of vital importance to them, it takes a nontechnical, human approach that may illuminate their own experiences.

CHAPTER 1

Introduction

Psychology has been much concerned with the study of fear and anger. This preoccupation is understandable, since these emotions are so often the sources of human problems. Those theorists who deal with mental health, especially, have been active in centering attention on anxiety and hostility as factors in stress and conflict. An unfortunate result of this concentration of interest has been the neglect of other important emotional states. "The positive emotions," writes a psychologist, "love, joy, hope, courage, were either entirely ignored by theorists, or, in the case of love, treated as the expression of the sexual instinct . . . As a result, the sentiment of human love has been practically unexplored . . ." (Arnold, 1960, I:228).

This book is in large part an effort to repair this neglect, and especially to explore the esthetic and emotional aspects of sexual attraction. It had its genesis some years ago when, while teaching a university course in human relationships, I encountered some questions concerning sexuality for which clear answers were lacking. The questions were in a region of emotional experience beyond the usual meaning of sex, and concerned feelings definitely unlike those of sexual arousal. Answers were not to be found, moreover, in the current literature on sex psychology.

There was fair agreement in this literature that there is a kind of emotional attraction between man and woman that differs markedly from the feelings and impulses associated with physical intercourse. Commonly called sexual *love,* this attraction was conceded to be different in quality from those involving the sex organs.

From this basic premise a number of questions arose, however, on which there was little or no agreement. How does this kind of love differ from "sexual desire," and how are the two related? Is love of this kind essentially the same as the common feeling of concern for the well-being of another, sometimes called "tender-protective," or is it a separate emotion? Here the books on sex psychology failed to reach an accord, both as to whether there was a difference, and, if so, what it was.

It is certain that people are much more discriminating about "falling in love" than about accepting a sex partner; the standards are much higher for the one than for the other. Theorists do not agree, however, on what makes one person more attractive than another, or how this kind of choice differs from that made on the basis of sexual desire. Important questions are left unanswered—or are poorly answered—concerning the origins of sexual preference and why people often differ greatly in their choices.

What Determines Sexual Choice? Some Answers

The *range* of answers for questions like these in the literature on sex psychology is remarkable. Sexual love, for such authorities as Sigmund Freud and Havelock Ellis, is closely related to sexual desire in its commonest meaning, has the same source, and is simply a different form of expression of the same urge, a change brought about when satisfaction is delayed. While Freud regarded the love between man and woman as a sexual motive, he fully recognized its unlikeness to the desire for intercourse since he believed that a *conversion* (called ".sublimation") must occur to account for the marked difference in experience (Freud, 1922). There will be no love if the physical impulse is immediately gratified; it develops only if the impulse is blocked; there must be restraint, or inhibition. The entire experience of "falling in love"—the adoration, tender affection, admiration of charming traits ("beauty") —he saw as a product of the change of sexual desire into other kinds of feeling. In his psychology, the emotion with which this book is primarily concerned would not exist but for the many checks which nearly all societies have placed between the basic impulse and its natural goal.

For another eminent student of sex psychology, Theodore Reik, love between man and woman, far from being closely related to sexual desire, is not even in the same category (Reik, 1944). It belongs to an entirely different mental realm: that of the *ego,* ego needs, and especially ego frustration. In its peculiar denial that "sexual" love is really sexual at all, Reik's view illustrates the great differences in theory in this realm of emotional experience. Before a person can fall in love, he thinks, there must be dissatisfaction with the self, low esteem for one's personality, and a desire for better traits and qualities. Attraction and love begin when we meet someone who exhibits some of the traits we long to have: this person represesents to some degree the ideal self, whatever the ideal happens to be; he or she becomes a kind of substitute fulfillment of needs of this kind. The longing, possessive aspect of sexual love Reik regards as in reality the desire to *own* the attractive individual; to possess the desirable traits which the lover himself lacks.*

The adoration so characteristic of sexual love in its traditional romantic form is, in Reik's view, really an envious admiration of the idealized personality. When one has won the beloved, one's personal goals are fulfilled; one is a completed self. The *choice* of a love object is easily explained by assuming that the chosen person happens to have the qualities which meet the needs of the potential lover.

The views of Freud and Reik, then, differ sharply; and a third founder of modern sex psychology takes yet another approach. Albert Moll, a contemporary of Freud, proposed that human sexual makeup consists of two entirely distinct components (Moll, 1924). One impels toward genital pleasure; the other is expressed in an experience of attraction which is *not* a mere by-product of inhibition, but an independent sexual motive. The second impulse is most clearly seen, he suggested, in preadolescent boys and girls who find themselves fascinated with each other without any thought or feelings of physical sexuality. Attractions of this kind may occur long before puberty, Moll

* A recent writer offers a curious inversion of Reik's egoistic theory in the proposal that the experience of being in love results from the encounter with someone who *sees in us* the person we ourselves desire to be (Blau, 1972). One discontented with himself is perceived by another as having achieved his own ideal —which must of course be very gratifying. One may fall in love "at any time that another individual . . . gives evidence that the individual in question is acting in a manner which reflects the ideal image." Only an egoistically frustrated person, thus, can fall in love. The process is admitted to be a "very complex human interaction." This, among other reasons, would make it hard to reconcile with features of amorous attractions in early childhood, an objection which also applies to Reik's theory.

believed, and may become quite strong. Eventually, with maturity, "sensual" feelings normally enter into such attractions, but the first experiences may be entirely free of these feelings.

Long ago an American student of sexual behavior, H. T. Finck, wrote two large volumes on his observations. In one of them, called *Romantic Love and Personal Beauty* (Finck, 1887), he laid the basis for an *esthetic* theory of sexual emotion. Like Moll, he made a clear distinction between sensual desire and sexual love, and was solely concerned with the latter. In his view, attraction included a number of feelings and impulses, the strongest and most important being the response to personal beauty. Sexual love he defined as a "pure esthetic sentiment," and devoted nearly half of his first volume to an analysis of the esthetically attractive features of the human body.

While conceding the vital role of character and personality in the growth of the emotion, Finck made it clear that the physical features are foremost in arousing the "romantic" emotion. Other traits might influence its growth, but he believed that attractions of great depth and intensity might be born of a "flash of esthetic admiration." Being interested only in the nature of this experience, he did not even include the sexual impulse in his analysis. What is there, he asked, to excite sensual desire in an intriguing profile, a certain arching of the brows, the tilt of the nose, or the curvature of the lips? Our response to these charms, he felt, may be as free of sexual desire as our enjoyment of a sunset, a flower, or the graceful movements of a bird on the wing. Sexual desire is an "appetite." The romantic emotion develops out of admiration, or *adoration*.

The French psychologist Alfred Binet, renowned as the inventor of the intelligence test, was also greatly interested in the phenomenon of the attraction of the sexes. He too concluded that the romantic emotion is esthetic in origin and quite unlike sensual desire (Binet, 1887). He believed, that is, that there are two different kinds of human sexual response.

Binet's chief interest, however, was not so much in the emotion itself as in what makes one person more attractive than another to a particular individual. On the basis of certain observations he concluded that attraction is aroused by special physical characteristics; which characteristics attract varies greatly from person to person.

One of the principles of abnormal psychology is that a number of deviations and "peculiarities" appear to differ only *in degree* from normal behavior. Binet was struck by the similarity of certain unusual kinds of sexual interest, called *fetishisms,* to the varieties of normal attraction. The fetishist may find extraordinary sexual charm in a hand, a foot, in feminine hair, or in a quality of voice—among many other possibilities. He may be so fascinated by some feature as to disregard all else almost completely. It occurred to Binet that such peculiarities might be simply extreme cases of the preferences seen in normal attraction —the latter, in other words, might be simply *minor* forms of fetishisms. If this were true, the study of fetishisms might provide a key to normal sexual choice.

Present-day writings on the attraction between man and woman offer little evidence that the difference between the romantic emotion and the sexual impulse is at all clear. Sometimes it is hard to recognize that the romantic experience itself is being described. Erich Fromm, for example, in his widely-read book *The Art of Loving* (1963), gives an authentic and memorable statement on parental and "brotherly" love. He rejects Freud's view that nonsexual affection, or "tender" love, is a converted ("sublimated") form of the sexual impulse. Yet the kind of emotion so familiarly known as "falling in love" he describes as essentially an experience of "sudden intimacy," a "sudden collapse of the barriers . . . between two strangers." As the strangers come to know one another better—an experience described as "exhilarating and intense"—the emotion subsides, and terminates in "the wish for a new conquest, a new love." Fromm characterizes the experience as a whole as normally very brief, an "explosive" episode.

I suggest that anyone who had ever known any degree of the romantic experience at first hand, or even read about it, will have difficulty in recognizing it in these phrases. They do not refer to esthetic interest, do not explain why the amorous passion has been linked for so many centuries to beauty. Fromm does not tell us why such intimate encounters should be "exhilarating and intense" simply because barriers to personal knowing have been removed. He does not even tell why they should involve a member of the opposite sex, since the only essential seems to be the experience of intimacy. Finally, he bypasses the fact that sexual love, like personal knowledge, may grow gradually—it is not always or necessarily "explosive."

If Fromm's statement seems inadequate at least it concedes the reality of an emotional response which may be sudden and intensely exciting and which yet is not the same as the sexual impulse. Dr. Rollo May, in another widely read book, *Love and Will* (1969), does not even include this emotion in a roster of meanings of the word "love." His list includes (1) the sexual impulse; (2) a "drive to procreate or create—the urge toward higher forms of being and relationship"; (3) friendship, or Fromm's "brotherly love"; (4) "love devoted to the welfare of others."

Here again the reader may wonder if his experience of a deeply moving emotional response to a person of the opposite sex could be fully described as motivated by "procreative" or "creative" impulses. May's definition seems to me even less fitting as applied to the kind of amorous fascination seen in preadolescent children, for example, as will be illustrated in some of the material to be presented later.

Dr. Karl Menninger, in a section on love in one of his books, states that in "mature sexuality . . . the attraction is between personalities as a whole, not merely between parts; hence the functions of the genital organs are . . . no longer the principal expressions of love." He suggests, in other words, that love, unlike sex, includes the whole person. The statement fails, however, to distinguish *kinds* of sexual behavior or *qualities* of the related behavior. To say that in love the genitals are no longer the "principal" means of expression, is to imply that only a shift in emphasis has occurred. One might easily infer that the feelings are pretty much the same in either case.

Dr. Menninger further observes: "The world's greatest lovers have not been Don Juans and Casanovas, but Schweitzers, Gandhis, Helen Kellers, and such saints as Francis of Assisi. It is a common misconception of psychoanalysis that it disrobed love and showed it to be something carnal. . . . what psychoanalysis showed was that true love is more concerned about the welfare of the one loved than with its own immediate satisfactions . . ." (Menninger, 1963, p. 365). Here our comment must be that reserving the term "true" love for the feelings concerned with the welfare of others—granting the supreme importance of such feelings—is not justified if it implies that *sexual* love is somehow a less genuine or authentic emotion,—perhaps even that it is not worthy of the name of love. The romantic experience may differ in kind from altruistic feeling without losing its reality. Fortunately the common reference to being "in love" as a synonym for the sexual emotion reinforces its right to the label. It may, in other words, be "true" of its type or kind.

The Nature of Sexual Love

This book attempts to distinguish not only between the sexual impulse and sexual love, but also between sexual love and nonsexual affection. Psychology often neglects to make the latter distinction, confounding love and affection or treating them as different aspects of the same emotional state.

A professor of psychology, for example, writing of the child who "falls deeply in love with his parent of opposite sex," describes this love as a "passionate emotional need," also as "frankly sexual in intent and aim." Accordingly, the child develops intense jealousy of the other parent, just as an adult lover does when his possessive urge is threatened. Likewise the child—"inevitably," we are told—develops the fantasy of some day marrying the parent. "This is the natural human way for little boys to prepare to grow into men who can love women, and for little girls to prepare to grow into women who can love men" (Cameron, 1963, p. 69). Since the emotional normality of the adult depends on such experiences in childhood, it follows—so this writer suggests—that a person will probably never develop the ability for mature love if for any reason he or she does not fall in love "passionately" with the opposite-sex parent. In the same vein, the writer regards the love of the parent for the child as essentially sexual too, but as a converted or "sublimated" kind of sexual desire, expressed only in "warm tolerant affection."

The notion of sublimation cannot account for the growth of sexual love, as we shall show at a later point. When two emotions are unlike in quality and when their expressions also differ in significant ways, we think they are to be regarded as different emotions, rather than as different forms of the same emotion. The difference between the emotional attraction of adult lovers and the tender-protective feelings and impulses of those who love but are not "passionately" or sexually aroused will be illustrated in Chapter 2. That both emotional states may be expressed in physical contacts or caresses, moreover, is not ground for regarding the feelings as identical or similar. One of our contentions will be that adult "romantic" passion and the affectional response of a young child to its mother are different emotional states and that it is misleading to say that a child is "in love" with its mother if this is likely to imply the same experience as that of mature passion.

The mood associated with amorous emotion may at its height be a truly exalted state, a "peak experience," which gives a freshness and new coloring to almost every field of awareness. It is greatly augmented when the response is mutual. The experience of being fully accepted by a highly valued person meets important needs other than those of the sexual sphere itself. The loved one may feel a notable lift in morale and a general expansion in the enjoyment of living.

The accounts of this mood are sometimes inflated, however, to the point where realistic description is lost in cloudy metaphors and phrases suggesting transformations of personality or even levels of "being" beyond the natural order. The amorous state—again according to Dr. Rollo May's *Love and Will*—is, among may other things, "the drive toward union with what we belong to—union with our own possibilities," union with another in whom "we discover our own self-fulfillment." It is "the yearning in man which leads him to dedicate himself to seeking . . . the noble and good life." It is a mode of relating to another in which we seek to "procreate and form the world" (May, 1969, p. 74–75).

For another student of the "romantic phenomenon," what lead us into love is "an impatience for our basic, eternal, supernatural condition—both germinal and final." Love is, in essence, a "love of fatality"; it "consecrates, makes divine," is a sacred state of being (Lilar, 1965). Still another writes: "In the ecstacy of romantic love a new quality is struck; existence is elevated into the eternity of interpersonal fulfillment." It is a form of "existential transcendence" (Sadler, 1969, p. 167).

The amorous state, in a mature individual with a well-developed capacity for it, may be deeply moving and have stimulating and expansive effects in other regions of the emotional life. These effects may easily be exaggerated, however. Many of the phrases employed by Professors May and Sadler, by Suzanne Lilar and others with a bent for the poetic and metaphysical, could not possibly be applied, for example, to the quite genuine amorous responses of a 12-year-old or even a fairly mature teenager. A valid account of this emotional state must at outset be fitted to all who have experienced it, and must therefore be focused on its common and essential elements. It will have different meanings for different people, and for those of different ages. At one end of the scale the response may be so weak as to make little more than a minor overtone to physical sexuality, while at the other it may project into thoughts of transformation of the personality, elevation into "spiritual" realms, predestination, and so on. The meaning of the experience, as a later chapter will show, has varied greatly from one age and society to another. Whether it is merely marginal to the sexual impulse or something semi-mystical and touching upon the divine depends largely on the social context in which it occurs and upon the emotional temperament of the person concerned.

Inflated descriptive language may, of course, be permitted to the lovers themselves and may well express their experiences, but it is not the language of psychology. The emotional exaltation of the romantic state may "create a new world" while it lasts, but this cannot be regarded as distinctive of the experience. The achievement of a long-sought goal, the discovery of a new truth, or the more or less sudden accomplishment of almost any kind, in major dimension, may evoke similar states of exaltation and markedly color the mood.

Why Study the Romantic Experience?

Given the great differences among the major sexologists as to the nature of sexual love, I began to explore several fields: (1) the literature of academic and clinical psychology*; (2) biographies and autobiographies containing descriptions of the experience; (3) novels describing or expressing the psychology of attraction; (4) the findings of many years of work in the fields of clinical psychology, marriage analysis, and inquiry during premarital interviewing. The romantic emotion is surely worthy of better understanding in a society in which, more than in any other in history—sociologists tell us—it is regarded as the normal and necessary preface to marriage. At its peak, moreover, it is one of the most powerful emotions in the human repertoire. Whatever its nature, and however long or briefly it commonly survives the intimacies of marriage, its sheer potency warrants giving it a respectful examination.

*Some readers may note the relatively small number of references of recent date. Our study centers exclusively on the emotional elements in attraction. Samplings from current literature were thus limited to those of direct bearing on this neglected area of sex psychology; relevance rather than recency was the criterion governing selection.

Other grounds might be indicated for such a study, among them the possibility, at least, that of all human esthetic experiences this kind of attraction is the most basic and the most frequent. It is the "music of life," as someone has said, for those who may be otherwise tone deaf, the one great lyric note in the emotional experience of a great many people. Countless novels and "half the poetry of the world" should be evidence enough that falling in love is worthy of understanding.

CHAPTER 2

The Amorous Emotion

Most books on sex psychology, at or near the beginning, describe the anatomy of the sex organs and the way they function. They discuss sexual desire, impulse, or appetite, and explain the different methods of erotic arousal, with suggestions as to the most effective stimulation. The ways in which men and women differ in their sexual attitudes and responses are defined. Such books leave no doubt as to what *kind* of sex is meant, that is, no question as to which of the several meanings of the word is intended. The center of discussion is sexual intercourse, and the final goal in every phase of the subject is sexual pleasure and satisfaction.

"Sex" may have a very different meaning, however, and there is a quite different kind of sex psychology. It begins not with sex anatomy but with the fact that men and women are *attracted* to each other. Part of this attraction is, of course, sexual "desire," but there are other important ways in which they attract each other, and for different reasons.

Men differ from men, women from women, very little in their sex organs, but they differ enormously in sexual attractiveness when the entire body and personality are considered. This must mean that there is a great deal more to

14

the psychology of attraction than the sex organs and their activity. It is to the phenomenon of attraction between man and woman that the early chapters of this book are devoted.

The experience of attraction in mature men and women usually includes some degree of sexual desire or "appetite," but it may also include an emotional state which is often a larger part of attraction than the desire for genital contact. Since this emotional state may become a deeply moving and intense experience, we will need to define it or at least describe it. For this purpose the best examples are found in early adolescence, and in instances in which genital-sex interest has not yet fully developed.

Here a young college student describes his first strong attraction at the age of 12:

> I had picked up some scattered information about sex by this time, rather lurid and not very appetizing, but I had never thought of any particular girl in this way and I am sure I had never been sexually stimulated by a girl. I had never masturbated and I was only mildly curious about sex.
>
> Yet it was at this time that I had one of the most memorable and exciting emotional experiences of my life. The cause of it was a girl in my 7th grade classroom. For an entire year I was *fascinated*. I was conscious of her a large part of the time, and so much that it definitely affected my schoolwork. The attraction was mainly visual, her face and her hair, but her voice, when she recited in class, was thrilling too. I was too shy ever to approach her and I was "spellbound" whenever she came near me.
>
> I can remember longing to be with her, and very jealous when I saw her with other boys. I clearly recall feeling a painful kind of ache when she once walked home with a friend of mine. *But mainly I remember her face,* which I thought was extremely beautiful (I'd

have said "pretty" at the time). I watched her in the yard during recess and thought about her often away from school, with plenty of day-dreaming.

I can still recall her features very clearly, but very little about her "figure." I am positive I never thought of her sexually. Since then I have experienced the same kind of attraction to other girls, though never quite so absorbing. But the main difference, of course, is that I've become much more conscious of sex.

This account of youthful experience illustrates some characteristics of a kind of emotion aroused by a person of opposite sex that is obviously quite different from what is usually meant by the term "sexual." The emphasis here is on visual fascination with the *facial* features (apparently with little interest in the rest of the body); on desire to be near, with some evidence of *possessiveness* (inhibited by timidity but expressed in jealousy); and on continuous *preoccupation* which lasted through the school year, and terminated only when the girl transferred to another school. Despite the remarkable strength of the attraction, the youth is quite sure that genital-sex interest was absent.

In a later part of his sexual history this young man referred to attractions in which he experienced this kind of emotion as "love affairs," but he did not use this expression in referring to girls who only excited him sexually. The love affairs might, however, include sexual excitement as well as the emotion first experienced at the age of 12.

The account shows that what is commonly called sex attraction can have two different meanings: one, the most basic and familiar, is sex desire, or appetite; the other is usually called "being in love." In this book it will be called the *amorous* emotion. It is a different kind of experience in important ways.

Sexual Desire vs. Sexual Love

Some of the differences may be outlined. To begin with, sex "appetite" can mean desire for sex activity without any particular person in mind. It is true that it may be stimulated by a particular person, but—more important at this point—it may also begin as an internal urge that impels an individual to search for satisfaction in advance of such stimulation. A youth who feels this urge may "go out looking" for a girl, or he may go to a house of prostitution. What he seeks is an experience. He does not need a stimulus to prompt his seeking. A hungry man in search of food is similarly driven by an inner urge—the greater his hunger, the less it will matter what food he finds, and this is likewise true of the sex appetite. This kind of urge from within is best seen among those lower animals who become sexually active only at certain seasons, governed by the rhythms of body chemistry.

The amorous emotion is a quite different matter. It begins not as an appetite but with an *encounter,* not with *any* member of the opposite sex, but with a particular person. To speak of someone as "in love" is to say at once that he is emotionally fixated on one person. The amorous emotion is first and foremost a specialized kind of attraction. It means that a choice has been made, that a preference has been felt.

It is at high intensities that the difference between the two motives is clearest. The sex impulse at its peak is notoriously low in discrimination (illustrated, for example, in seafaring men after a long period of deprivation: almost any woman suffices; or in penitentiaries, where even the difference between the sexes may cease to matter). In this respect it may be compared with hunger, or perhaps with the craving of the alcoholic who may accept even a distasteful liquid if it contains the chemical he must have. But a person much "in love" would say that no substitute is conceivable, that no one else could possibly satisfy the desire he is experiencing.

Although both sex desire and the amorous emotion may be compelling when fully aroused, the total motivating power of amorous desire is by far the greater. A person who deserted his family or abandoned a career (or a throne) "for love" might be thought romantically reckless but certainly not necessarily unbalanced; but if he did so out of sexual compulsion he would surely be seen as a victim of pathology. People of both sexes have been depressed to a suicidal degree over broken love relationships, but it is doubtful that frustration of the sexual impulse alone could distress a mentally normal person to such a degree.

The sex organs have never been esteemed for beauty. Artists with pornographic tastes have drawn them, but they have not been included in esthetic appreciation of the human figure, and for reasons apart from considerations of moral decency. Freud noted their lack of esthetic value, and was perhaps a bit puzzled by it, since he traced the response to beauty, in animal evolution, to sexual stimulation (Freud, 1938). The fact remains that while human beauty has by vast consensus a great deal to do with sexual attractiveness, our response to beauty in the opposite sex is altogether different from our response to the sex organs.

While during moments of sexual excitement the genitals may be visually enjoyable in their own right (just as a steak might be described as a "fine sight" by a hungry man), such pleasure is very different in kind from that of a lover's appreciation of his sweetheart's face, or from that of an artist (who would no more think of painting the genitals than the steak as an object of beauty). The difference is very important for sex psychology, as will later be shown. We note it now only to underline the point that the attraction to human beauty is not only unlike sexual desire, but that it is closely related to the amorous emotion.

The two motives differ further in the tempo of their phases. Sex desire is quickly arousable, especially in the male, and also quickly terminated; there is "a tension, a spasm, and a release"; the desire is extinguished in the sexual act. Although an attraction that leads to an amorous fixation may in certain instances be an immediate response, the emotional arousal itself is typically a growth process extending over a period of repeated contacts. Its extinction, also, is slowly progressive; one grows out of love as one grows into it. Apart from exceptional cases in which strongly negative feelings suddenly appear, love does not drop, like sexual desire, from high intensity to zero. In addition, as one writer has noted, "Sensual pleasure becomes extinguished when satisfied, whereas love continues unabated, indeed, is enhanced the more satisfaction a person derives from another" (Symonds, 1946, p. 549).

Love as Affectional Need vs. Love as Attraction

A popular story—possibly a fiction—of a few years ago told of a lonely young girl who left a note, in a place where it might be seen, with the message: "To whoever finds this: I love you." The pathos of the tale lies in the image of one so much in need of someone to love that it mattered little who the object of her longing might be.

The story illustrates one popular answer to the question: why do people fall in love? It assumes that a love relationship *begins with a need*. Impelled by this need, the love-hungry person will then seek someone who will provide satisfaction, that is, someone he will be able to love, and who in turn may find him lovable. According to the view illustrated in the story, it is the need that is crucial;

the identity of the loved one does not much matter. It is implied, perhaps, that almost anyone with at least a minimum of physical appeal and personality will suffice. When the seeker of love finds such a person, the process of "falling in love" must supposedly occur because of the sheer emotional readiness of the lover.

But according to another view of the way the amorous emotion (or "sexual love") begins, it *does* matter what the other person is like. It assumes, in fact, that unless a special kind of person is encountered the process will simply not occur at all. One does not, moreover, look for someone to fall in love with. There need be no love-hunger that predisposes a person or causes him to be seeking someone, consciously or unconsciously. What triggers love is rather an unsought encounter with a person who is in some way unusually attractive. Certain physical or personal traits will be crucial. *Individuality* of some kind is the essence of the appeal: the lover perceives a striking individual difference that attracts him or her to the loved one.

The word "attraction" itself, in fact, suggests an effect produced by an external agency. It is true, of course, that a hungry man could say that he was "attracted" to food, but a parallel to amorous attraction would be a person who discovered a new and unusually tasty food, to which he then became strongly addicted. The youth in our earlier illustration emphasized how exclusively he was drawn to a particular girl because of the very special charm of her facial features. In line with this view of the meaning of attraction is the well-known preoccupation of people "in love" with certain traits and qualities of the loved one, who is typically regarded as irreplaceable *because* so "different." Since people differ so greatly in physical attractiveness that it is nearly always possible to choose among them, it seems highly probable that such preferences are related to the kind of fixations we are examining.

How are we to choose between these two very dissimilar

accounts of the way falling in love begins? Is the truly basic factor an inner need, or an outer influence? Is hunger the better analogy or is attraction more like hearing an intriguing musical melody and wanting to hear it again and again?

We suggest that there is no real dilemma here simply because two essentially unlike experiences have been taken to be identical. The problem arises only when they are confused, that is, when one is mistaken for the other. Both are called love and are assumed to involve people of opposite sex. Since both are usually expressed in embraces and in terms of endearment their confusion is understandable. Yet the underlying emotions are different, and therefore should have different labels. One of them will be called *affectional* need, the other, *amorous* emotion. The latter is sexual, in that typically it is aroused by people of opposite sex. The former is not sexual, and is not an "attraction" in the usual sense of the term. It may be expressed toward persons of either sex. It is different in origin and in quality as an experience.

Affectional need begins in early childhood. Some students consider it inborn, but more often it is regarded as a result of the infant's utter dependence on others and of the association of affectionate treatment with the satisfaction of physical needs. Affection and the feeling of security and well-being therefore become closely linked. The child continues to have a desire for affection from others; he very early shows "a desire to receive and an impulse to bestow affection." The close connection between satisfaction, security, and affection is so strong that it is never outgrown and is very nearly universal. "Every individual has tendencies to *receive* which spread to wanting to be loved, to receive affection, to belong to the group . . . These tendencies are recognized as basic . . ." (Symonds, 1946, p. 38).

Receiving affection from others therefore becomes a

symbol of *being loved*. Feeling sure of being loved is what is commonly meant by emotional security. "This need for security is not something that is felt only in infancy when one is helpless and when loss of love would be a real threat; this need continues all through life" (Symonds, 1946, p. 35). The need of affection is so vital that the lack of it in infancy has been found to retard the growth process itself; "emotional hunger is an urge as definite and compelling as the need for food."

It should be at once apparent that this kind of need, when mutually experienced by persons of opposite sex, explains the kind of behavior seen in one type of love relationship. The following statement by a girl of twenty, married for two years, is illustrative:

> I was very unhappy at home. Both my parents worked, but we were never a close family anyhow. I had felt lonely for a long time. I began to date Herbert because one of my girl friends wanted me to. He wasn't much to look at and it sure wasn't a romantic affair but he seemed lonely, like me. I began to feel that he needed me and I felt good when I could make him happy. For a while after we were married I was happy too. He was affectionate and the sex part was all right but sometimes I'd feel more like a sister to him and sometimes even like a mother. During the second year I began to feel like I had missed out on something. I don't think you could say I was ever really in love with Herbert. I was just very fond of him.

Many marriages and love relationships are of this kind. This does not mean, of course, that the factor of attraction need be absent altogether. A relationship may include amorous emotion as well as affectional need, but the latter may be much more prominent. Such instances give rise to the familiar observation that an emotionally dependent youth is seeking a "mother image" in his wife, or that an immature girl is "looking for a father" in her husband. In the example just cited there was very little amorous emotion, but much affectional need on both sides.

In the contrasting type of relationship the emphasis will be quite different. There will be much greater stress on physical charm and "sex appeal." Each person finds the other exciting to be with. There is a tendency to dwell on esthetically attractive traits, on mannerisms, and *style* of personality. The quality of the relationship is "romantic," with the accent on glamour. An example:

> There was a timbre or a kind or resonance in her voice that affected me so much that sometimes I would hardly follow what she was saying. Then there was the way her brows were arched, with one higher than the other; and the way she moved about, always smooth, with a certain grace about her. I know these things were very important in the way I felt about her, although I realized that character is supposed to be a lot more important. Is this what is meant by infatuation?

In its "purest" or least complicated form, amorous behavior is best seen in attractions of the grade-school years. They are, first of all, selective: an individual girl or boy stands out from others because of certain characteristics. These tend to be surface traits, the focus of attention most often being, as in our first example, a distinctive marking of the facial features—the richest area of physical individuality. Attraction is expressed mainly in visual preoccupation: the boy watches the girl, wherever she is; he notes everything she does. In conversation with her it will be evident that his interest centers more upon *her* than upon what she says. The tendency of such interest is always toward closer approach, eventually to come into contact; the final goal is some form or degree of embrace.

In a study of the amorous behavior of grade-school children it was observed that some form of embrace was the most common emotional expression (Bell, 1902). Possessiveness and jealousy were in evidence. The otherwise sociable child would abandon his playmates to devote himself exclusively to the chosen one. Physical attraction entered into the preferences even among children under the age of eight, the prettier ones (girls) being more often the object of attention. The strength of attraction was evident not only in the behavior described but in the expression of grief during separations. Only in exceptional cases was there any indication of genital-sex excitement.

Affectional need may be the bond between friends of the same or opposite sex, as well as between parent and child, and between siblings. It may be just as genuinely *felt* between adult males, but in our culture the expression of such feeling is limited by custom to handshakes and shoulder pats. If we think of sex interest in terms of the object alone, it is clear that this kind of feeling is not sexual, nor does it become so when it develops between man and woman. This is simply to say that there can be nonsexual affection between persons of opposite sex, or that love between the sexes need not be *sexual* love. Much confusion in the use of the word "love" can be avoided if the distinction is kept in mind.

Many of the traits that cause people to experience affection for each other are also nonsexual in the sense that they are common to both sexes. When a man says of a woman: "I love her because she is unaffected, loyal, generous and zestful," he is obviously not loving her as a member of the opposite sex; he might value a male friend for the same reasons.

Our interest being in *sexual* love, we shall be concerned with a quite different kind of trait: those, namely, that make the difference between males and females and cause them to attract each other sexually. The most apparent ones are, of course, those of physical structure and include the entire body, with the facial features as the richest area of individual variation. Attractions also center on the voice, qualities of movement, carriage, and mannerism, and certain differences in courtship behavior.

The traits or features referred to here are commonly classed as *esthetic*. The emotional responses they arouse are quite different in quality from those of "sexual excitement." They are much more like the feelings associated with the appreciation of art, and especially of music. It will be our thesis that "falling in love" is the direct and progressive effect of repeated responses to traits of this kind.

Three different motives that impel men and women toward each other have been placed in focus. One of them needed little discussion, being the commonest and most basic meaning of sex as seen throughout the animal world and so well-known as to need no further treatment here. Another is not a sexual motive, being experienced toward persons of either sex and expressing emotional needs probably traceable to infancy.

The third is usually or normally directed towards persons of opposite sex. It is sexual because of the kind of emotion associated with it, because of the traits that arouse this emotion, and the impulses that follow the arousal. It is this motive which will be the subject of most of the book.

In mature love relationships the sexual impulse and amorous emotion tend to become closely merged. They are, nonetheless, so unlike that it can be said that human sexuality includes two components, and that there are two different meanings of the word "sex." In an older way of speaking it might be said that there are two sexual "instincts." In referring to one we speak of appetite and sensuality; while for the other people are said to be enamored, adoring, captivated, and so on. The differences are great enough to convince a few psychologists that the two motives have separate roots. Theodor Reik, the author of several books on the subject, regards the differences as "of such a decisive nature that it is quite unlikely they could be . . . of the same origin and character" (Reik, 1944).

Granted the dissimilarity, the question of the connection between them immediately arises, since both are involved in attraction. It has been answered in widely different ways. One of the most accepted explanations denies, at outset, that there are in reality two kinds of sex and holds instead that there is but one truly basic impulse, and that all other forms of sexual behavior, however different they may seem, are no more than indirect or transformed expressions of the same source-motive. For a statement of this point of view we turn to one of the founders of modern sex psychology.

Love as Sex Transformed: Havelock Ellis

The writings of Havelock Ellis, a contemporary of Sigmund Freud, cover many different fields of sexual behavior. He contributed importantly to the effort to remove, early in this century, the taboos against the study and discussion of this behavior, and helped to bring greater candor into the public attitude toward it.

Ellis recognized the difference between sexual impulse and amorous emotion and had an explanation to offer regarding the connection between them. He believed, however, that an understanding of human sexuality must begin with the study of its simpler forms. This meant getting down to the bed rock of biology to determine what sex

means in the animal world. From these studies he concluded that there is but one fundamental meaning of the attraction of the sexes to each other, and that is, solely and
essentially, the arousal of the desire for genital coupling.*
No matter how far from this goal certain kinds of attraction and behavior seem to be, and however little they
might seem to be related to it, there was no question as to
what they were for: all were but erotic stimulants, preliminaries to the sexual act. Ellis was emphatic about this basic
unity of sex throughout the whole of nature. It may seem a
long leap "from birds to man; yet . . . the phenomenon
among primitive human peoples, if not, indeed, among
many civilized peoples also, closely resembles those found
among birds . . ." (Ellis, 1936, p. 41).

Ellis considered two views of the brilliant coloring of
birds and the melodies of their songs. One was that they
have an esthetic sense and are attracted to each other in
the same way in which certain patterns of color and sound
are attractive to people. The other was that "beauty" or
"charm" as we understand them have no meaning at the
lower levels of life, that the colors and sounds of nature
are no more than a direct stimulus to the physical mating
impulse. Ellis did not hesitate to decide in favor of the
latter view: however esthetic the courtship behavior of
birds—the dramatic displays and maneuvers—may appear
to us, it is all no more than a progressive incitement to the

* Ellis saw the key to sex psychology in both man and the
lower animals in what he called "sexual courtship." This was a
name for everything related to the building up of the desire for
intercourse through stimulation of all of the senses and for every kind of behavior designed to excite desire (Ellis, 1936). An
example in which he was much interested is the often dramatic
displays and maneuvers of mating in certain lower organisms,
especially the birds.

act of mating.* He went further than this, however, and in keeping with his animal model, he denied that the response to beauty is important even in human attraction. "Love springs up as a response to a number of stimuli . . . the object that most adequately arouses the sexual impulse being that which evokes love; the question of esthetic beauty . . . is not in itself fundamental and need not even be consciously present at all" (Ellis, 1937, III:V).

In line with his emphasis on the behavior of the lower animals as the key to human sexuality, Ellis devotes many pages to the senses of touch and odor as agents in the arousal of the impulse. He found, however, that vision is primary at the human level; accordingly he gives a long treatment of the different standards of attractiveness among various races and nations, and here again the issue of esthetics appears. The sex organs, he concedes, are not beautiful, yet the sight of them may be highly exciting when the sensual mood is aroused. The human face may, on the other hand, be very beautiful, and Ellis grants that the response to this kind of beauty is different from that to the genitals, but fails to consider the meaning of this difference for the emotional aspect of attraction. It is rather

---

* A biologist (Julian Huxley) who has closely observed the behavior of birds disagrees with this. "Anyone who, like myself, has watched such birds by the hour day after day must be struck by the fact of their enjoyment of the courtship ceremonies for their own sake, and the further fact that the ceremonies are often what we may call biologically self-exhausting, in that the birds' emotional tension is often liberated through them, instead of being stimulated and leading on to actual pairing. It would seem as if these strange and romantic displays . . . constituted a bond between the two birds . . . binding them together so long as the breeding season lasted by emotional links" (Huxley, 1927, pp. 201–2).

curious that he can say that "the love thoughts of men have always been a perpetual meditation on beauty," and elsewhere conclude that the essential purpose of beauty is to stimulate sexual desire.

In approaching *human* love Ellis was finally forced to abandon the animal model and to admit that many expressions of love in man are so unlike those of animals that some transformation must have occurred. How does the sexual impulse become sexual love? Knowing that they are not the same, but assuming that one must come from the other, Ellis could only conclude that the impulse somehow *changes* into love through the workings of the nervous system, the basis of mental activities. Since no factual knowledge was available, he could only venture a guess as to what occurred; he suggested that the nervous processes basic to sex must take different pathways to explain why love is a different kind of experience from sexual desire. In his own words, the sexual impulses spread "through the whole organism, taking larger nervous circuits and suffusing regions which lie outside the sexual sphere so long as the sexual impulse attains its ends speedily and without impediments" (Ellis, 1946).

Love as Sublimation: Sigmund Freud

A notable part of the statement just quoted is the idea that sex becomes love by a change brought about by obstacles. If the impulse reaches its goal "speedily", love is not aroused. Only if desire is blocked in some way is the emotion generated by a spreading of nervous currents.

This view comes very close to the widely-accepted principle of *sublimation,* which in its older usage meant change of a substance into a more refined, higher, or more spiritu-

al form.* Applied to the mental sphere it was well fitted to
the difference between sexual desire and "romantic" love,
since the latter is commonly regarded as a more elevated
feeling than sensuality. For Ellis it meant a real emotional
change brought about by a process neither willed nor conscious. It was not assumed to occur in everyone, however,
some persons being limited to direct sexual expression and
incapable of the romantic attitude and feeling.

The idea was further developed by Freud. He emphasized the checking of the sexual impulse as the condition
for the change of one desire into another. The amount of
amorous emotion (of being "in love") depends on how far
sexual desire has been inhibited (Freud, 1922). To explain
how a person may experience both sensual and amorous
feelings at the same time it was only necessary to suppose
that some of the basic impulses were sublimated and that
some were not. Inhibition may not be complete and assumedly is rarely so.

One of the nonsexual meanings of love was discussed
earlier: an affectionate, "tender" sentiment, often expressed in some form of embrace (and therefore often
confused with sex). Since this sentiment is commonly present in sexual love, Freud regarded it as a product, like the
amorous emotion, of inhibited sexuality. (Freud, 1922)
However lacking in erotic feeling such affectionate impulses may seem to be, they are rooted, he believed, in the
sexual impulse. The process of sublimation is thus supposed to be capable of literally changing one desire into

* A recent example: "sublimation is in no way the renounce-
ment or repudiation of the principle of love; to *sublimate* is not to
deny . . . it is . . . to restore upon a higher level; not to condemn
but to glorify. . . . Sublimation is a peaceful effort to achieve
nature's work in us, that of perpetually raising up the lower by
causing it to participate in the higher life" (J. Guitton, *Human
Love* [Chicago: Franciscan Herold Press, 1966] 91).

another. This change in the *quality* of experience is accompanied, moreover, by another and different kind of change: the tender affectionate love-feeling is usually much more lasting than sexual desire, and this greater duration is seen as a further result of the sublimative process. The sexual impulse vanishes with physical satisfaction, but under restraint or blocking it becomes the source of *lasting* affectional attachments (Freud, 1922, pp. 118–19).

Still another element of attraction is brought into the same formula. The response to beauty is interpreted as also a product of sublimation, which here again can convert one emotion into another. The difference in quality between the response to the sex organs and to facial beauty was stressed earlier. Freud suggests, nonetheless, that one is derived from the other: sensual desire, with its appetitive response to the genitals, undergoes change, when inhibited, into appreciation of the esthetic values of the body.

If there is in reality but a single source of the several different kinds of emotions indicated, sublimation would be a truly remarkable process. It has been at any rate a very popular idea, and many examples of its use in sex psychology could be quoted from the literature of psychology and sociology, especially during the period when Freudian concepts were accepted less critically than at present. Thus: "sublimation of sex emerges under conditions of separation of the sexes and the presence of other obstacles to freedom of association between them. . . . In American culture . . . a great body of behavior, artistic, recreational and religious, are substitutes for sex expression" (Burgess & Locke, 1945, p. 374). Some statements were more specific and blunt: "in romantic love the lovers are at once aroused and inhibited sexually. This state of conflict evokes the disturbing emotion known as 'being in love,' . . . the more strongly an individual is excited by sexual stimulation and the more completely this biological urge is frustrated, the greater will be his emotional disturbance" (Young, 1943, p. 379). A prominent literary figure raised the query, regarding the decline of sex morals, as to what could be done "to create those internal restraints without which sexual impulse cannot be transformed into love" (Huxley, 1930).

The doctrine owed its popularity not only to the prestige of Freud and the fact that it appeared to solve the problem of amorous emotion, but because it was well fitted as a support for morality by offering a way to release sexuality in "higher" forms than that of the physical outlet. The impulse being convertible, more approved ways of expressing it were available.

Is Sublimation a Reality?

The doctrine may be tested in several ways. Is there, for example, evidence of similar conversions in other human emotions?

If change in the quality of experience is a primary feature of the sublimative process, it may be questioned whether it occurs in the case of other basic emotions such as fear and anger. Anger may be discharged in indirect ways and is often transferred from one situation to another in the form of a mood, but the experience itself remains unchanged except that the indirect expressions may be milder in degree. A person may not understand *why* he is angry or hostile in a given instance, but he will know that he is experiencing these feelings.

Fear seems a likelier possibility since it is well known to be remarkably versatile in attaching itself to objects far from its source. It may even be free of linkage to any definable threat, in this form being termed "free-floating anxiety." But fear and anxiety differ mainly in their sources. They cannot be said to differ in quality of feeling, as do the sexual impulse and amorous emotion.

Sublimation clearly fails to account for the negative variety of esthetic reaction. The perception of unattractiveness ("ugliness") is as basic as that of attractiveness, or "beauty." Aversion to physical traits is an equally real experience and is in the same esthetic mode. It is not clear how one and the same process can account for exactly opposite reactions.

The sexual impulse, like hunger, has a rhythm rooted in body chemistry; it is one of the "appetites." Both urges impel to specific actions and subside when these are completed. What would sublimation mean if it were applied to hunger in the same manner as it has been applied to the sexual impulse to account for amorous fixation? We would have to imagine a hungry person in search of food, and to assume at outset that he would have some sort of preference. Suppose further that on finding his preferred food, but for some reason being unable to consume it, he became exclusively absorbed in his craving for it, losing interest in all other foods. Such a fixation would hardly be seen as ordinary hunger and would doubtless be regarded as an abnormality. Yet the same interpretation has been widely accepted in the case of sexual love.

In reality both hunger and sex become *less* selective when satisfaction is denied and as desire increases. The food preferences of a starving man will soon be abandoned and he will finally accept almost anything edible. The sex impulse, strongly aroused, becomes increasingly less discriminating. Falling in love by sublimation would appear as extraordinary as our imaginary food fixation, with blocked desire becoming strangely rigid instead of normally flexible. This would suggest that sexual need, unlike others, changes into a different kind when blocked. The alternative is to conclude that "one cannot sublimate starvation nor a distended sex-gland"—as one psychologist puts it—and seek another way of explaining sexual love (Allport, 1937).

Societies with unusually permissive standards for sex behavior should provide another source of evidence. The writer has elsewhere reviewed some cases of this kind, with special reference to the people of the Trobriand Islands (Grant, 1957).

These natives of northwestern Melanesia were among the few primitives who placed little restriction on sex activity. Young children engaged freely in sex play, and intercourse was permitted as soon as physical growth made it possible. This freedom continued into adolescence, during which couples paired off and lived together. Opportunities for sexual satisfaction were plentiful. "Not only need no one live with impulses unsatisfied, but there is also a wide range of choice and opportunity" (Malinowski, 1929).

Early attractions tended to be shallow and brief, but during adolescence they acquired greater depth. Choice and the fixation of preference were increasingly in evidence; attachments became more enduring and possessive. Liaisons showed increasing strength as the boy and girl matured, and finally an attachment included a desire for permanence. The important finding, for our interest, was that *emotional fixations* developed despite the unlimited sex freedom of the partners, and that they were sustained by personal attractiveness alone, without external pressures, since a couple could separate at any time. The investigator found "what we ourselves mean by love: . . . steadfast preference and repeated attempts at possession. In many instances there is a pronounced appreciation of the personality loved, and of its power to enrich life or leave it empty" (Malinowski, 1929, p. 318).

Amorous and erotic interest, in this society as in our own, were focused upon the head and the features, the quality of the voice, the symmetry and grace of the body as the most important elements of attraction. Marriage was prompted by the desire for a home and children. Social status and economic gain were incentives as well, but the desire to possess the beloved person with a lasting tie was often the foremost motive. Despite complete sexual freedom, nearly everyone married.

In brief, it appears that strong emotional attachments based on selective attraction developed in the entire absence of the restraints supposed in Freudian theory to be basic to sublimation. The descriptions of the amorous behavior might very well fit our own society but for one feature: the romantic attitude, the mood of idealization and mystery—the aura which we would perhaps call "glamour"—was here absent. It was apparently dispelled by the easy physical intimacy and the fact that in such small social groups the attachments involved people who might have grown up together and knew each other well. Glamour and mystery require something of the unknown and unfamiliar as stimuli. An attractive stranger is better material for fantasy than the girl next door.

If primitive people in general were found to have more sexual freedom than societies like our own, and if amorous fixations commonly developed among them, the case for sublimation would be clearly damaged. However, the sexual freedom of the Trobriand Islanders, while by no means an isolated case, is not typical of primitive people, nor are the fixations characteristic of such societies. The Trobriand case stands, but no general conclusions can be drawn from it.

A better argument can be made, in fact, for a quite different statement: that restriction, taboo, and disapproval of extramarital sex activity is widespread among the "simpler" peoples, some of them being almost Victorian in their attitudes. In the majority of instances studied, restrictions of some degree are placed on sex activity and often these are rigid, with severe penalties for violation. "The taboo is always in evidence; it would appear sometimes as if both the primitive and the more developed human society had expended most of their energy in dealing with the sex relation, so numerous are the varieties of restriction which are to be found . . ." (Sumner, 1929, III: 1568). Such taboos may operate as effectively to check the sexual impulse as the moral code or fear of disapproval, disease, etc., in our own society.

A study of 120 primitive social groups revealed that cases in which sex activity among the unmarried was disapproved were about equal to those in which it was permissible (Hobhouse, Wheeler, Ginsburg, 1930). Other surveys have furnished similar findings. The common notion that "savages" tend to be promiscuous is false, and many instances have been cited of severely restrictive attitudes. Of the people of New Guinea, Margaret Mead writes:

> The whole picture is one of a puritan society, rigidly subduing its sex life to meet supernaturally enforced demands. . . . Dress and ornamentation, removed from any possibility of pleasing the opposite sex, becomes a matter of economic display and people only dress up at economic feasts . . . An hibiscus in the hair is the sign of magic-making, not of love-making. The village lies fair in the moonlight, the still lagoon holds the shadow of houses and trees, but there is no sound of songs or dancing. The young people are within doors. Their parents are quarreling on the verandas or holding seances within doors to search out sin. (Mead, 1930, p. 173–74)

If in many of the simpler cultures the sexual impulse is subjected to the kind of checking necessary for sublimation, there should be a corresponding amount of amorous attraction and the kind of behavior commonly associated with it. Yet in fact sexual love as we know it is not a general feature of primitive behavior nor has it been reported with frequency. It is easy to find, in the studies reported, statements to the effect that "love between a man and a woman is not a phenomenon of uncivilized society." One student observes that it is rare "to find a tribe where romantic love is appreciated"; another, that amorous emotion among primitives is occasional but not lasting or deep. It has even been suggested as a general rule that the lower the level of a culture, the less likely is the emotion to be found. A widely quoted statement in this context is that the rarity of strong emotional attachments in most human groups means that they are not to be regarded as normal behavior:

> all societies recognized that there are occasional violent attachments between persons of opposite sex, but our present American culture is practically the only one which has attempted to capitalize these and make them the basis of marriage. . . . Their rarity in most societies suggests that they are psychological abnormalities to which our own culture has attached an extraordinary value . . . (Linton, 1936, p. 174)

Among studies of specific peoples, Margaret Mead has reported that romantic love as we know it, linked with exclusive possession and jealousy, does not occur among the Samoans. Of the natives of New Guinea she writes: "There is no word for love in the language. There are no love songs, no romantic myths . . ."

It is important, however, to acknowledge the exceptions, the individual cases among people who may not generally exhibit the amorous fixation. There are numerous reports of this kind. An anthropologist comments on a tale from American Indian folklore: "It contains all the elements of romantic love." While not citing it as characteristic of primitive life, he regards it as "not an isolated instance by any means" (Sapir, 1930, p. 365). References to romantic love often occur in the folklore and myths of a people, if not in their reported behavior. A student of Indian culture finds evidence of this kind among the myths of various tribes: thus "the concept of veritably romantic love repeatedly crops up in the folk-tales of the Crow Indians" (Lowie, 1935). There are other and similar reports, pointing to the conclusion that though primitive people do not "fall in love" as much as we do, the difference may be essentially one of frequency and degree.

The evidence briefly outlined is clearly not favorable to the doctrine of sublimation. It has not been demonstrated that one motive can be changed into another in the way assumed. There may be large differences in the modes of expression of an emotional state. An angry man, unable to directly punish an enemy, may indulge in vengeful fantasies or write a letter charged with emotion, or verbally vilify the person to others, but the quality of the feeling remains the same. A woman denied the satisfaction of motherhood may express her "need to be needed" with animal pets. A sexually frustrated individual may enjoy talking or reading about sexual pleasures or indulge in fantasies. But these are differences in outlet rather than differences in desire. They are not comparable to the differences between the sexual impulse and esthetic enjoyment of sexual beauty, or to the difference between sexual desire and the love felt by a parent for a child, or by close friends, or by husband and wife when sexual needs have been satisfied. Like other organically rooted needs, physical outlets appear to be essential to release of sexual tension. Freud himself conceded that "a certain degree of direct sexual satisfaction appears to be absolutely necessary for by far the greater number of natures" (Freud, 1933,II:83).

"True" Love

A distinction was made earlier between sexual love and "love between the sexes." Language usage sometimes marks off the first by reference to being in love. The kind of emotion termed love between the sexes, or simply, non-sexual love, has a much broader meaning. It is a bond between any two persons regardless of sex, or of relationship, or between a human being and an animal.

Often called "true" love, it is what is usually meant when speaking of "loving" a person and is something altogether different in quality from sexual desire or from esthetic attraction. Its essence is *concern for the well-being* of another. When present between man and woman it is essentially nonsexual; it may accompany sexual feeling and even blend with it, yet remain distinct. It may be prominent in a close friendship. It is the central emotion felt by a mother for her child.*

In current literature in this field the most common definition of sexual love regards it as composed of sensual desire and the "tender-protective" impulse. Here we differ from other sex psychologies in that we regard sexual *love* —the amorous emotion—not as tender, protective or unselfish, but as a possessive, essentially egotistic emotion.

* A student of emotional evolution writes: "It has been almost universally assumed that feelings of tenderness and affection are part and parcel of the attraction between the sexes. That attraction is commonly spoken of as 'love,' and the sentiment is identified with the sexual impulse" (Briffault, 1927, I:117). Close though this association may be, he stresses that this kind of love is not an inherent part of the sexual relationship. True love, in its traditional sense, is not basically included in attraction. In the animal world from which we came the sexual impulse is more often associated with brutality than with anything like tenderness.

The male enamored of the esthetic charms of a female desires, first and foremost, that she *belong* to him, that he may own and enjoy these charms for an indefinite period. Of the two kinds of love, thus, the nonsexual is self-giving and sacrificing, the sexual is self-centered, "acquisitive," and jealous or anxious when possession is threatened.

The workings of jealousy support our view. Jealousy is commonly regarded as a selfish and therefore unworthy human sentiment, and legitimately so in the context of true love as we have defined it. In sexual love, jealousy has a different meaning; a lover incapable of it is under suspicion of being no lover at all. Jealousy is inherent in sexual love as a natural reaction to threat of loss.*

Much has been written of the fundamental source of true love. The writer's experience during many years of marriage analysis and study of family interaction confirms the view of those who regard *maternal feeling and impulses* as the prototype of concern for and response to the needs of others. Whether, as some have suggested, this kind of concern is an expanded evolutionary development of the maternal "instinct" is of less moment, but it would be a consistent inference.

* One of the writer's clients in marriage counseling charged that her husband's objection to her dancing with other men at parties was selfish, depriving her of an innocent pleasure. If he "truly" loved her, she felt, he would be glad to permit her this harmless enjoyment. The conflict was seen in a different light by her husband, the history of the marriage having proven, he was sure, that she could be attracted to other men to a dangerous degree. He had demonstrated in many ways that his wife's happiness was important to him, that his love was unselfish; it was only when his possession was in jeopardy that he expressed his anxiety in the protests which she regarded as selfish.

Two unlike kinds of love were here confused, one inherently possessive, the other normally solicitous and generous.

Early in the century a student of human social emotions proposed that "the same tender emotion and the same protective impulse (which are the essential manifestations of the parental instinct) are elements in the normal love of man for woman" (McDougall, 1926, p. 560). He saw it as the important part of all love, with the ancient observation that "pity is akin to love" as one of many ways of saying that the tender-protective impulse and emotional response to those in distress are the universal core of the human love sentiment.

"Loving" is, of course, a matter of degree, and in its milder expressions may be called fondness, altruism, "friendship love," or simply "social feeling." In the latter sense another of the greater psychologists, Alfred Adler, proposed that woman's maternal nature as expressed in solicitude for her children is closely related to the feelings underlying all sentiments of fellowship for others, whether related or not. "The biological heritage of social feeling is entrusted to her charge. . . . It may readily be accepted that contact with the mother is of the highest importance for the development of human social feeling. . . ." (Adler, 1938, p. 214). A student of human emotional origins suggested that love as affectionate solicitude began with the mammalian female; that tender impulses of this kind "are one and all derivatives of the maternal instinct and products of female evolution." (Briffault, 1931, p. 498). The maternal emotion is "very much more primitive, fundamental and stronger than . . . love . . . in the relations of the sexes." Maternal love is the original source of *all* emotion of the same quality.

Among mammals the parental relationship is mainly that of mother and progeny, the paternal role being relatively limited. Maternal feeling gradually extended to include the mate; the capacity for it was finally transmitted in various degrees to the males of the species. "Just as the

transferred affection of the female for the male is a derivative of maternal love, so likewise all feelings of a tender,
compassionate, altrusitic character are extensions and
transformations of the maternal instinct and are directly
derived from it" (Briffault, 1931, p. 513). An anthropologist who has given much thought to this area of the emotional life believes that woman's *humane* impulses,
essentially an expression of her maternal nature, are the
source of all that mankind has developed in the direction
of altruism and fellowship feeling. "The love of a mother
for her child is the basic patent and model for all human
relationships. . . . to the degree to which men approximate
in their relationships with their fellow men the love of a
mother for her child, to that extent do they move more
closely toward the attainment of perfect human relations"
(Montague, 1958, p. 157). In her capacity for caring, woman's maternal impulses are the root of all that is sympathetic and unselfish in human interaction. An historian,
writing of the origins of morality, finds that human *ethical*
awareness first arose out of the emotions central to family
life. Our highest moral values, which include the love of
others, "were not anywhere upon our globe until the life
of father, mother and children created them." (Breasted,
1961, p. 410). Biologists have likewise observed that the
group life of social animals is largely an extension of family behavior.

Finally, references to "true" love which imply that there
is a less valid variety of the same name can be misleading.
Sexual love, or amorous emotion, is not only a fully authentic experience but at its peak one of the most powerful
human feelings. Its reality is grounded on esthetic characteristics of the sexes which are no less tangible than those
of the larger field of esthetic responses in general. Sexual
love is a *true* love, but of a different kind from that whose
prototype is the maternal emotion.

The many uses of the word "love" make a rich field for semantics. The writer has been impressed, during many years of marriage analysis, with its different meanings in dialogues between people who assumed they were referring to the same feelings. For one man who "loves" his wife, for example, it may mean chiefly concern for her welfare and sympathetic participation in her emotional life, while for the wife it may express mainly a dependent relationship, her love for her husband being her need of him and for the affection that enables her to feel secure. It is usually a matter of emphasis rather than of sharp distinction, but the differences may be large enough to account for some of the failures in communication and in understanding. They may also be slow in emerging. Thus: "I was forced to conclude, after nearly twenty years of marriage, that when she said 'I love you' it did not mean the same as when I said it." A more common instance, the wife speaking: "When I thought of my love for my husband I never had sex in mind, but it was usually during intercourse that he told me he loved me."

Love and Friendship

How does sexual love differ from *friendship?* The word covers a variety of attachments. One might use as a baseline a relationship grounded upon a shared activity, as when co-workers react to each other in terms of a common interest. Interest in the person himself may then be small, and any positive feeling toward him may be focused in reality on the common objective; one reacts to *it* rather than to him. Similarly one may respond positively to a person who is simply entertaining, or informative, etc., without *liking* him.

Liking may be said to begin when traits are revealed which are universally valued; for example, helpfulness, naturalness, or a pleasing mannerism ("I began to like him because of his amiable smile"). Friendship in the most usual sense is associated with some degree of affection or "fondness," which in turn conveys concern for a person's well-being and the impulse to respond to his needs.

Whether such feelings are aroused will depend upon factors on both sides of the relationship. There must be traits or emotional states that arouse concern or solicitude, as well as capacity for such responses. An individual of "strong" personality, who impresses one as highly competent and self-sufficient, is less likely to arouse them than someone who is perceived as vulnerable to distress. This does not mean that a person must be weak in some way to arouse solicitude, but rather that a degree of need is most likely to arouse sympathetic or compassionate feelings and impulses.

How, finally, does sexual love differ from such relationships? The question is often encountered among young people who are unsure of the meaning of falling in love, and feel a need to distinguish it from "mere" friendship or affection.

We propose that insofar as attraction to another is motivated by shared interest, or by behavior traits which do not differentiate the sexes (humor, enthusiasms, qualities or contents of the mind), or by feelings of affection rooted in sympathy or compassion, the emotion is not amorous. When in any of these relationships there enters a feeling that is aroused by pleasing surface characteristics that are structural or behavioral (tone, manner, personal style) and when attraction of this kind leads toward closer physical contacts, the experience is amorous, regardless of any other emotional responses, or in their absence, and regardless of the sex of the persons concerned.

We now return to the basic question: Is there only one

kind of sexuality, with transformations, or is this too neat a view of the varieties of sexual behavior? The attempts of Freud and of Ellis to trace the whole of sexual behavior to a single motive being in our view unsuccessful, a radically different approach may now be considered.

CHAPTER 3

The Growth and Expression of Amorous Emotion

Theory of Albert Moll

Albert Moll, a contemporary of Freud and Ellis, was the chief founder of the doctrine that there are *two* sexual motives, different as experiences and different in origin and development. He based an important part of his sex psychology on the appearance of personal attraction at an earlier age than genital-sex interest. This chapter will present and examine the kind of evidence on which he based his view of attraction.

Moll pointed out that the sexual impulse may be independent not only of amorous attraction but of *any* sexual object. Self-stimulation may occur as a solitary act, without the agency of even an imaginary partner. In this sense the impulse is not basically social at all. Self-stimulation occurs in many of the males of lower animal forms, and this even though the female may be available. It appears to be natural behavior.

Moll observed that boys and girls may be attracted to each other long before the sexual impulse becomes directed toward another person. Boys might be masturbating, for example, during periods of attraction to girls, but without evidence of sexual arousal in the presence of girls or of any sensual interest in them. They might be drawn toward contact and embrace with girls yet remain free of genital excitement. As they matured, contacts were increasingly likely to include such excitement, but as early as age seven or eight, boys experience attractions with several features of adult "romantic" fixations without genital-sex interest.

Numerous examples of Moll's view can be found in the literature on the growth of emotions in children. In some of these, children were found to be attracted to one another before the age of puberty or of sex interest; this attraction manifests itself mainly in visual fascination and the impulse to approach. Moll observed that with maturity the two elements of sexuality tend to merge, at times closely blending, and often varying with now one, now the other dominant. His work was carried further by others, with frequent stress on individual differences in the relative strength of the two kinds of sex interest. Capacity for amorous emotion may be small in comparison with the intensity of the sensual impulse. A person with weak genital sexuality may, on the other hand, be strongly moved by amorous feelings. Women, Moll believed, tend to be more often inclined in this way than men.

A number of other students, in essential agreement with Moll, have pointed out differences between the esthetic attraction of the sexes and "sexual desire" in the physical sense. Differences in both the emotional experience and in the resulting behavior have been noted.

Among the studies based on a two-factor view of sexuality, several of the features of amorous emotion noted earlier have been emphasized. Its tremendous power, far greater than that of the sexual impulse, has been stressed. "It would be quite ridiculous," writes one, "to think that if men die for the love of a woman whom they are unable to possess, it is because they have sought of her, in vain, a small bodily sensation which the first woman who comes along would be able to give them" (Binet, 1887, p. 260). The esthetic factor—*the response to personal beauty*—has been seen as the central element in amorous attraction. Equally important is the fact that this response is a highly individual affair, and that a person attractive to one may arouse little interest in another. Human individuality is here at maximum; the endless variety of tastes and preferences run parallel to the enormous range of differences in physical structure. (Few phenomena in nature, it has been said, are more remarkable than the infinite number of possible combinations and modulations of the features of the human face.)

A few observers have been impressed by certain differences in the objects of amorous and genital sex interest. Studies of children reveal that it is rare for the same person to be the source of both kinds of attraction. A small boy may be "romantically" interested in one little girl, and engage in sex play with another, but seldom exhibits both types of interest in the same person (Bühler, 1931). Evidences of preference, moreover, are more prominent in amorous attraction than in sex play, doubtless reflecting the fact that sex-related parts of the body vary much less than the facial features. Finding a sex partner, almost anyone would say, is easier than finding someone to love.

The difference in quality between the two kinds of interest have often been noted. Amorous impulses are satisfied with the *presence* of the loved one, and with prolonged close contact. The impulse toward sexual contact, on the other hand, introduces a perceptible change of emotion, a "shift of gear" with a different and further goal. The reverse may also occur, and Freud observed that with a high degree of amorous feeling, "tendencies whose trend is towards directly sexual satisfaction may . . . be pushed back entirely, as regularly happens, for instance, with the young man's sentimental passion . . ." (Freud, 1922, p. 75).

In accounts of amorous emotion the esthetically attractive trait is emphasized. The response is similar to artistic appreciation of the body in terms of pleasing contours and movements, to the colors and tints of the skin and hair, and to the intricate charms of the complex of the facial features. There may be special reference to the voice, which has been compared with fingerprints because of its highly individual nuances.

In the quite different *sensual* mood there will be less attention to grace and proportion, more to the body parts provocative of sexual interest. It is granted, of course, that some features may bring out both kinds of response; the difference lies in the *kind* of feeling aroused rather than in the stimulus itself. The voice, for example, whose pitch and timbre are primarily musical for one person, may be primarily sensual for another.

As for the amorous experience itself, many theorists have tried to account for the traditional distinction between "true" love and a supposedly less genuine, less stable emotion labeled "infatuation." Both are conceded to have great potential intensity. Writers on sex have proposed that "infatuated" attractions are those that are immediate and that tend to be associated with *surface* traits having a special charm. "True" love, by contrast, is less externally stimulated; it tends to embrace the entire person and personality and to include deeper-lying traits of character. Whereas infatuation suggests an emotion which springs up suddenly and may perhaps as readily subside, "true" love develops more slowly but is more enduring.

Finally, modern studies have stressed the selective feature of attraction, finding the key to sexual love not in sublimation but in something perhaps so familiar that it is often overlooked: the phenomenon of *choice*. Sensual desire, to repeat, may be strong before a choice is made; it becomes less concerned with choice as it grows. Amorous emotion *begins* with choice, becomes less responsive to competing attraction, becomes more and more exclusive as it grows.

Research Supporting Two-factor View of the Sexual Impulse

So much for theory of sexual love and its relation to the sexual impulse. We still must consider some of the evidence on which such views are based. Here we are handicapped by the meager amount of systematic research available on amorous behavior. Nothing like the Kinsey surveys has been focused on the emotional side of the sex relationship.

In a pioneer study of the behavior of several hundred boys and girls of grade school age, the children were observed in settings in which they could freely express sexual interest in each other (Bell, 1902). Amorous attractions appeared long before puberty and were evident in children under ten in much the same manner as in adults. The children attracted were attentive to each other and often seen together. The goal of this interest was an embrace or some degree and kind of contact. They sought each other out, talked and walked together. There was "hugging and kissing," confession of feelings, gift-giving, jealousy, distress at separation.

Intense possessiveness was noted, preoccupation with the loved one and withdrawal of interest from friends and acquaintances. Physical attractiveness was a factor; the prettier girls were more often the objects of attachments. The observer of this behavior was convinced of its amorous character in part by direct evidence and in part by the testimony of adults who reported on their experiences of attraction in childhood. Evidence of sexual excitement in the usual sense of the term was rarely noted; it was concluded that amorous-esthetic attraction in childhood is almost entirely lacking in physical arousal. "In love between the sexes at this early period . . . the physical sensations of sexual excitement are generally wholly wanting, or if present are entirely unlocated" (Bell, 1902, p. 333).*

The findings of Arnold Gesell (1946) on children studied at the Yale Clinic of Child Development include observations reported by parents. The child of *seven* may experience an "elementary love affair." He reports pairing between boys and girls to be fairly common at this age, particularly in the school setting. As in the earlier study, it is noted that such attractions and attachments are suggestive of "rudimentary love affairs," implying resemblance to those of adults. There are "engagements" and marriage planning, with occasional evidence of deep feeling when the loved one is lost. At age eight the "romantic note" is observable: "Boys recognize a pretty girl, and girls choose handsome boys . . ." (p. 177). At nine such interests persist despite the tendency of the sexes to segregate at this age.

G.V. Hamilton (1929) collected data on early amorous

---

* Sanford Bell's study, here summarized, included 800 cases observed over a period of 15 years. He also collected 1,700 reports by adults of early love experiences. He gave examples of his material but no numerical data. Though crude in method it remains the most comprehensive research of its kind, and its conclusions have been confirmed by later investigations, which have been smaller in extent, though better controlled in method. Freud (1938) was familiar with Bell's study and conceded that sexual *choice* accompanied by strong emotion could occur in childhood as early as age five. Robert Sears (1943), in commenting on Bell's work, observes that it provided a more factual and realistic account of sexual behavior in the early years than Freud himself ever offered.

behavior as reported by 200 adults, evenly divided between men and women. His findings confirmed those of others concerning the earlier age of amorous attraction as compared with genital-sex interest. Of his feminine samples 38 percent experienced the first love affair between the ages of six and eleven, but 95 percent reported no awareness of sex desire before puberty. The reports from men were similar, but with fewer (two-thirds) denying sex desire for these years. As to the earliest amorous attraction after puberty, two-thirds of the women and 69 percent of the men reported this experience to be free of conscious sex desire. The earliest experience of attraction, according to Hamilton, is not that of the genital-sexual impulse.

A specialist in the psychology of childhood considers the preadolescent to be fully capable of the romantic attachment. "At the elementary school age and even before, many youngsters are tenderly devoted to a boy or girl friend and go through acts of courtship, such as bearing gifts or walking together to and from school." (Jersild, 1968, p. 296). However short-lived, such attachments appear to be quite genuine during their course.

Many examples of the independence of amorous-esthetic attraction and the sexual impulse appear in the literature of emotional development. A few of these may be indicated here to show the separation of the two forms of sexuality during the course of growth, both before puberty and during the teen years. To any adult who has experienced the emotion there is little novelty in examples of this kind, since its early "symptoms" are surprisingly similar to the later ones. The expressions mature but the affective quality appears to be fairly constant.

A representative example follows:

> For several years during the late teens I had fantasies about girls, usually at night before falling asleep. I

often imagined having a sex affair with a girl. Most of the fantasy had to do with the preliminaries leading up to the act, and quite often I fell asleep before this climax. These fantasies were all sex. The girl's face was pretty much a blank, but I thought a good deal about what sort of body she would have. Usually I got an erection. Sometimes I would feel in a different mood and then there would be no sex at all in the fantasy. I would imagine a very beautiful girl with the kind of personality I admired, and imagine meeting her and courting her. Mostly I would picture her face and her voice and the things we would say to each other. The end of these was always that I would propose to her and we would embrace. There was never any sex in these fantasies and they never gave me an erection. I would sometimes have trouble to decide which kind of fantasy I would have, depending on how I felt. When I was having a romantic one there was never any temptation to bring sex into it. The two things just didn't mix.

Among the case histories collected by Havelock Ellis (1936), the following are illustrative of the experiences of amorous emotion in the absence of genital-sex elements, or of their separation when both are present. Each selection (paragraph) is from a different subject:

I can distinctly remember from the age of 9 years, and am sure that I had no sexual feelings before the age of 13, though always in the company of girls. I had many boyish passions for girls, always older than myself, but these were never accompanied by sexual desires. I deified all my sweethearts, and was satisfied if I got a flower, a handkerchief, or even a shred of clothing of my inamorata for the time being. These things gave me a strange idealistic emotion, but caused no sexual desire or erection. (I, 2:290)

54 *Falling in Love*

At 12 he fell deeply in love with a girl of corresponding age. He never felt any powerful sexual desire for his sweetheart, and never attempted anything but kissing and decorous caresses. He liked to walk and sit with the girl, to hold her hand, and stroke her soft hair. He felt real grief when separated from her. His thoughts of her were seldom sensual. (I, 2:280)

I fell in love and enjoyed kisses, etc., but the mere thought of anything beyond disgusted me. Had my lover suggested such a thing, I would have lost all love for him. But all this time I went on masturbating, though as seldom as possible and without thought of my lover. Love was to me a thing ideal and quite apart from lust, and I still think it is false to try to connect the two. (I, 2:300)

Looking back over the whole period of his youth and adolescence, he can trace the psychological effect of what was going on secretly, in his relations to girls and women. In a word, these relations were sentimental only. He hesitated to regard in any sexual way any girl of whom he had a high opinion; sexual desire and "love" seemed for him to inhabit different worlds and that it would be a pollution to bring them together. . . . Yet night after night he could masturbate, his imagination glowing with visions of female nakedness. (I, 2:321)

In my more idle moments I elaborated erotic day dreams in which there was a peculiar mixture of the purely ideal element, which never fused in my experience, but held the field alternately or mingled somewhat in the manner of air and water. One person usually served as the object of my ideal attachment, another as the center round which I grouped my sensual dreams and desires. (II, 1:236)

Another example shows, in sexual fantasies, the "two

worlds" of imagery corresponding to the "two kinds of sex":

> In late boyhood and early youth I was subject to an enthusiastic partiality for young girls of my acquaintance, with all the extravagances common to this youthful enthusiasm. But it never occurred to me to connect the world of my sensual thoughts with these pure ideals. I never had to overcome such a thought; it never occurred to me. This is the more remarkable, since my lustful fancies seemed . . . in no wise vile or obnoxious. This, too, was a kind of poetry with me; but it was divided into two worlds—on the one hand was my heart, or, rather, my esthetically excited fancy; on the other, my sensually inflamed imagination. . . . . In dreams the two spheres of my erotic ideas recurred alternately, but never combined. Only the images of the sensual sphere induced pollutions. (Krafft-Ebing, 1908, pp. 118–19)

One student collected cases of individuals distinguished by evidence that the genital-sex impulse was weak or absent, but with well-developed amorous responsiveness.

> A young man of 28 years, with apparently good heredity, seeks medical advice for his extremely weak genital sexuality. He denies ever having masturbated, has never experienced a desire for sexual relations. An experimental attempt at intercourse at the age of 20 failed through absence of sexual arousal; he is indifferent to the female genitalia. By contrast the patient is in no respect lacking in erotic inclination for the feminine; he is fond of being with girls, and has been in love several times; he feels a desire for embraces but no genital impulse. He is strongly attached at the time, and wishes to marry, but is restrained because of his sexual condition. (Loewenfeld, 1911, p. 152)

Havelock Ellis, a devoted collector of case histories of sexual behavior, himself supplied an item for our illustrative materials. In his autobiography (1939) he describes his "first love," a girl of 16, met when the future sexologist was 12 years old. She was a "dark, pretty, vivacious" girl who made an immediate strong impression upon him. He is emphatic that he took no "liberties" with her and that he experienced no impulse whatever of this kind. He writes that, following the separation brought about by circumstances,

> I never saw Agnes again . . . but for four years her image moved and lived within me. . . . I had no physical desire and no voluptuous emotions; I never pictured to myself any joy of bodily contact with her or cherished any sensuous dreams. Yet I was devoured by a boy's pure passion. That she should become my wife—though I never tried to imagine what that meant—was a wild and constant aspiration. I would lie awake in bed with streaming eyes praying to God to grant that this might some day be. (pp. 88–89)

Ellis adds that the experience awakened his esthetic sense: "I discovered the beauty of the world . . . a new vein of emotion within myself. I began to write verse . . . to enjoy art . . ." The effect of the amorous emotion was profound and pervasive; the "new ferment" affected his entire personality; it was "an epoch-making event." It may have been one of the factors that later led to his monumental study of sex psychology.

Many other examples could be taken from the literature of biography and autobiography. A classic example of early (eighth year) amorous experience is that of the poet Byron.

> I have been thinking lately a good deal of Mary Duff. How very odd that I should have been so utter-

ly, devotedly fond of that girl, at an age when I could neither feel passion, nor know the meaning of the word. And the effect!—My mother always used to rally me about this childish amour; and, at last, many years after, when I was sixteen, she told me one day, "Oh, Byron, I have had a letter from Edinburgh, from Miss Abercromby, and your old sweetheart Mary Duff is married to a Mr. Coe." And what was my answer? I really cannot explain or account for my feelings at that moment; but they nearly threw me into convulsions, and alarmed my mother so much, that after I grew better, she generally avoided the subject—to *me*—and contented herself with telling it to all her acquaintances. . . . I had never seen her since. . . . we were both the merest children. . . . .How the deuce did all this occur so early? . . . I certainly had no sexual ideas for years afterwards; and yet my misery, my love for that girl was so violent, that I sometimes doubt if I have ever been really attached since. (Quoted in Moore, 1832, I:26–27)

The difference between amorous and genital-sex attraction is well described in a boyhood experience reported by Max Eastman. The observation by Charlotte Bühler, that in childhood the amorous and sensual responses are typically not aroused by the same individual, is illustrated here.

I loved Ethel Marble from the time I saw her until we left West Bloomfield, and I love her still. But I believe I have never communicated with her except the momentous once when I handed her a little circle of white peppermint candy stamped with the words: "Will you be my sweetheart?" She brought me back the next day a similar circle of candy, colored with lime, and stamped: "You're too young and too green." It was all seemingly a joke, and I tried hard to make it so in my heart, but not successfully. There is almost always some single part or feature of a girl upon which your passion concentrates, and those mottled cheeks combining so miraculously with the wondrous beauty of her name—I trust you will have the courtesy to perceive its wondrous beauty—kept me in a state of sad poetics for a long time.

Side by side with that, and not a bit the same, I felt a lustful yearning over Nonnie Marlin. So did every other well-sexed boy in town, for notwithstanding her pimply complexion, there was a great power of attraction in Nonnie. Her round strong shoulders and round breasts and ease of attitude and action made her like a warm animal. She lived in a poor and tiny house four or five doors down the road from ours, and I never went by there without a forlorn casting down of eyes and a rising in me of the hot but hopelessly diffident desire to "put my arm around" Nonnie.

I did not dream that my two feelings toward these different girls might someday be focused upon one, and what a birth of the universe that would produce. A great many American boys of my generation—and boys everywhere, I guess—never do succeed in combining these two feelings, and that is one of the troubles with the life of love. (Eastman, 1948, pp. 80–81)

In a few of the sample illustrations above there is evidence, at least implied, of incompatibility and even conflict between amorous and sensual responses. The "spirit" of the traditional romantic state of mind appears to have been in some degree of disharmony with that in which sexual arousal was either dominant or under stimulation. One of the writer's subjects described this, in the context of esthetic response to a visual impression, as follows:

In a collection of pornographic pictures I came across one showing a girl with a very beautiful face lying with legs apart and her sex organ exposed. This picture affected me differently from all the rest. There was a kind of clash between her face and the sex part. It seems strange but I had the feeling that the two parts didn't belong together. I just didn't like to look at that picture. Such a pretty girl and such a rotten pose.

It seems improbable that there could be any basic conflict between the two sexual responses, since both attract men and women to each other and are at least biologically compatible in this sense. What we have here is rather a kind of esthetic disharmony. In states of sexual arousal the exposed genitals are visually enjoyable, whereas when the response to facial beauty is dominant, the essentially unbeautiful features of the organs may strike a dissonant chord in esthetically sensitive and perhaps romantically inclined persons. With a shift of *mood* from one state to the other, the conflict may be readily dispelled. Since, moreover, the amorous response escapes the taboos associated with sex, there will be for some people a decided difference in the feelings evoked. This is to suggest that the basic conflict is esthetic and that the difference may be reinforced when a moral judgment is made; society has very differently "defined" the basically unlike responses. Such observations serve, however, to further confirm that sexual psychology comprises two modes of experience and that these have been overlaid with other meanings and values.

CHAPTER 4

Individuality in Attraction: The Bases of Choice

A man on his way to a house of prostitution and a man calling upon his fiancée are both seeking members of the opposite sex, but they differ greatly in the value they attach to the source of attraction as an individual. One desires *a* woman, the other *the* woman. Amorous emotion differs from the sexual impulse in that it begins with a choice.

Esthetic choice is a fundamental of sexual behavior, seen in the lower animals as well as in very young children. Darwin (1874) observed sexual preference among domesticated animals. Birds show marked preferences, certain males being highly attractive for reasons unknown except insofar as courtship maneuvers, colors, songs, and so on may play a part. Darwin noted aversions as well as attractions ("likes and dislikes") in birds. Here preferences were seen mainly in the females, and in some instances could be described as "fascinations."

Konrad Lorenz (1962), an extraordinary observer of animal behavior, has reported the phenomenon of "falling in love" in birds and in mammals. Usually it occurs suddenly, at the first encounter. Examples are numerous among birds. That such attractions are more than the im-

60

pulse to physical mating is shown by the fact that they may precede it by a considerable period. "Among those few birds which maintain a lasting conjugal state, and whose behavior in this respect has been explored to the very last detail, the betrothal nearly always preceded the physical mating by quite a long period of time." (p. 171). Among the jackdaws "betrothal" occurs as much as a year before the species becomes sexually mature.

The likeness of animal courtship to that of human behavior is in some ways remarkable. There is play of the eyes; aggressive self-display of the males, who "show off" by challenging other males; the coyness of the female and her manifest gain in status among other birds when "engaged." More striking is the fact that the courting behavior is directed "always to one special female." The phenomenon of choice is clearly in evidence.

In his painstaking studies of a variety of goose Lorenz has observed very marked similarities between their behavior and that of man, finding that "highly complex . . . behavior, such as falling in love, strife for ranking order, jealousy, grieving, etc., are not only similar but down to the most absurd details the same . . ." The similarities in *expression* are so great, he finds, that the experiences must be essentially related to our own. In the display of grief when a mate is lost, for example, it is "almost incredible how detailed are the analogies we find here in human behavior and in birds."

In referring to "falling in love" among geese, Lorenz (1963) tells us that we do not need to use quotations marks to convey a difference between human and bird behavior. As with us, it may be sudden, and is clearly not the same as sexual behavior. Both man and geese behave differently in falling in love and in sexual excitement. The kinds of stimulation which release sexual (copulatory) behavior are definitely not those that evoke the strongest "amorous" attraction. Sexual and love behavior in these creatures may be as completely independent as they are in man, although they must finally combine upon the same partner if they are to fulfill their biological purpose.

The features of love behavior in this bird are complex and prominent, but "everything purely sexual plays a very subordinate role in the life of the wild goose." It is the love bond, and not sex, that holds the mating pair together for a lifetime.

Among anthropoids–chimpanzees, for example—sexual preferences and aversions are evident in both males and females. While man alone is capable of defining beauty and ugliness, "by their behavior animals of other species sometimes demonstrate an obvious preference for one type of sexual partner as compared with another" (Ford and Beach, 1951, p. 91). The resemblance is increased when we learn that, among the apes, some males are much more choosy than others, and are strongly attracted to certain females "with a particular facial appearance."

We do not know the basis of choice among the lower animals, and their behavior tells us nothing, of course, about human sex psychology. The simplest and safest view of choice among the animals is that it is based on *surface* traits of structure and behavior, such as the birds' response to color and movement.

At the human level as well the visual appeal of physical beauty is paramount in sex attraction. Surface traits are clearly primary in the appreciation of the features, the quality of the voice, or the character or style of movement. When a small boy is attracted to a girl because she is "pretty," it seems safe to say that he is responding to the shallow externals of appeal, and that choice at this stage of development is much the same as that of the lower animals.

Infatuation

In the human adult the phenomenon is of course much more complex. We need to know why attraction is sometimes immediate, sometimes gradual. We must know the difference between "infatuation" and "love at first sight" on the one hand, and a more lasting emotion of greater depth, on the other. Is infatuation always shallow and transient, or can it develop into "true love"? Is "love at first sight" something essentially unstable, or may it be the beginning of a strong and lasting bond? Is sexual love related to the familiar fact that one normally finds one person more attractive than another?

The answer may be introduced by way of some case illustrations. Here is a college student's account of an experience that corresponded to his idea of an "infatuation":

> I met this girl at a dance at a public ballroom. There must have been a hundred or more girls there, but few of them appealed to me very much, although a lot of them seemed to be pretty popular. I'm sure I couldn't have described what I was looking for because I don't think I had any particular type in mind. But as soon as I got a quick glimpse of this one girl in the crowd I immediately started toward her. There was no doubt in my mind that she was my choice. I danced with her, took her home, and started dating her regularly.
>
> I can say exactly what the big appeal was. It was in her eyes. Her brow line was high and arching, and there was a kind of fold in the inside corner of the lids that gave her eyes a slightly oriental look. I'm sure that nothing else about her affected me the way her eyes did. There was really nothing outstanding about her. She was not well educated or very interesting to talk to. Her figure did not appeal to me much. She

was too muscular to be quite feminine. We had sex
relations but I did not find her especially stimulating
that way. She didn't respond much.

The whole attraction was in those remarkable eyes.
The more I knew her, the less she appealed to me.
She was selfish and she exploited me. She could be
quite cruel, and sometimes very crude. I soon knew
that the relationship would not last, yet at the beginning I really thought I might have found the girl I
would marry. I knew, of course, that no marriage
could be based on a single attraction, and just a physical thing at that.

Note first that the attraction lay in a small structural
peculiarity, yet the emotion aroused was strong enough to
lead to thoughts of a serious commitment. The sexual impulse was clearly a minor factor here despite the power of
the esthetic appeal.

The case demonstrates that the central focus of amorous attraction can be located, that the person affected can
analyze the source of the emotion.

The next case involves specialized attraction to characteristics of bodily movements, in contrast with the sheer
"structural" element of the preceding example. A professional man in his forties writes:

I am very sensitive to the qualities of a person's
movements in walking. I can admire grace of movement in a man as well as in a woman, as in athletes or
ballet dancers. The shape of the leg is an important
part of it; the curves of the muscles must taper
smoothly; any suggestion of bulging or knotting is
repellent to me. But the character of movement is
what I notice, chiefly. I remember reacting strongly to
the walk of a matador in the arena, while watching a
bullfight. I thought his movements were so beautiful
that it distracted me from the contest itself.

But I react far more to the walking movements of a woman, and I give as much attention to her walk as to her face and figure. Recently I was much attracted to a very pretty woman in a business office and found her quite thrilling, but she almost completely lost her charm for me when she walked down a hallway ahead of me. Her legs were well-formed, but her hip movements were ugly.

Now to answer your questions: (1) my reaction to a graceful walk (that is, what is grace for me, or "my kind of grace") is like my feeling for a beautiful face. It is emotional, not sexual. I have never been sexually excited by a woman's walk, or certainly very little. I would compare it more with the effect of music, to which I also react very strongly. It is totally different from the way I feel when I'm sexually excited by a woman. It seems to me that I am quite normally excited that way, too. (2) As to falling in love I can say that I would rate the importance of a woman's walk as high as her facial beauty or as anything else about her that might appeal to me. It would be a very important part of what would make me fall in love with her.

On the other hand I doubt very much I could love any woman passionately if her walk was unattractive, no matter what I found desirable about her otherwise. Of course, I can't say it could not happen to me, but it seems doubtful. But I can easily imagine loving a woman with a beautiful walk, even if she were unattractive in certain other ways. Probably that sort of thing could lead to trouble, but that is the way I am.

Many people are stimulated by grace of human movement, of course; witness the devotees of the ballet. For many others, we can be sure, such spectacles are of little interest, while among ballet enthusiasts there will be a few who respond more intensely than the rest. The subject of our last example is therefore not unique in his esthetic

interest, but it is safe to say that he is unusual in the high
value he places on walking-movement quality as a feminine charm. (Not many men will follow a woman for
blocks, as he does, solely for this pleasure.) He is a "specialist" in his appreciation of one facet of the feminine. It is
important to note also that this responsiveness may be related to the arousal of amorous emotion.

Liking vs. Loving

One final example may help to make clear the difference between traits that relate to amorous emotion and
those that do not. Here the emphasis shifts altogether
from surface to "depth" traits.

My first marriage lasted about two years. My wife
divorced me for infidelity. I deserved it, and I've always regretted the way I hurt her, for I really cared
for her a lot.

Elizabeth and I met through our mothers, who had
just gotten acquainted and liked each other. They
decided we would "make a good match." I want to say
at once that I never met a nicer girl than Elizabeth.
She was friendly and kind, unaffected and intelligent.
Everybody liked her; she had a lot of friends. She was
fair-minded in everything, and generous. There was
just nothing really wrong with her. I had to agree
with my mother that she was a really fine girl.

But from the beginning I could never get really
excited about her when I thought of her as a wife. For
all her personality she did not have what I would call
feminine appeal.

When I first met her I felt let down. My mother
had met her before and had given me a build-up. I
had to agree about her personality, but that was about
all. She was not a plain or homely girl, but to me she
was simply not physically attractive. I don't mean sex-

ually, because her figure was all right. She just was
not the kind of girl I'd look at a second time on the
street. There was nothing exactly wrong with her features, no defects, but she did not have anything that
affected me the way a lot of girls have that I'd call
good-looking. There were times when I felt affectionate toward Elizabeth, but I never got a thrill out of
kissing her.

My mother would say "beauty is skin deep" and
character is what makes a marriage that lasts, that I'd
have a good companion and a good mother for my
children. She was right, I suppose, and maybe I was a
fool. I felt very guilty about hurting Elizabeth the way
I did, playing around with other women. I've never
met any girl I've liked and respected as much as Elizabeth. The trouble was simply that I was attracted a lot
more by other girls in a way that she never attracted
me. She never excited or thrilled me (except sometimes sexually) the way certain other girls did. I felt
badly about breaking it up, but there was something
missing from the beginning.

It is clear that in this instance the amorous emotion was
not aroused. There was "liking" and respect, but no esthetic attraction. There was "love" in this relationship in that
the subject was *fond* of his wife, concerned about her happiness and welfare, and truly remorseful for the distress
he had caused her. But apart from physical sex the attachment was essentially a friendship based upon the appeal of
traits which are always and everywhere valued in others.
This man esteemed his wife highly and experienced affectionate impulses toward her, but he was not "in love" with
her because she possessed none of the esthetic charms to
which he was responsive.

The marriage failed, not through conflicts and abra-
sions, but because the husband's need of an amorous relationship was frustrated. In consequence, he was too often

attracted elsewhere. With such attractions his wife could not compete despite her several assets. Had his emotional makeup inclined him to value the external features of the feminine less and the personality elements that make an enjoyable companionship more, the marriage might have continued in the absence of amorous feeling.

The first of our three cases presents the precise opposite of this one in the relationship between character and sex attraction. There the appeal, despite its strength, was almost entirely esthetic. Had there been personality traits of any importance, the outcome might have been quite different. It must be emphasized, however, that despite the shallowness of the attractive elements, the emotion aroused was of genuinely amorous quality—the subject was "in love," whereas in the last case the subject was not, regardless of the degree of his fondness, concern, and solicitude for his wife.

Such contrasting examples of the presence and absence of amorous emotion may parallel closely the popular distinction between liking and loving, or between liking and being "in love," often illustrated in such comments as "I'm in love with her but I do not like her," or "I like him very much but I don't think I'm in love with him," or, finally, "I'm not only in love with him; I like him too."

The difference between the two emotional states is easy to recognize when amorousness is fully aroused. *Liking* is "quieter" and less exciting; in its lesser degrees it might be questioned whether it is to be classed as an emotion at all. In reference to the amorous experience, on the other hand, such terms as "rapturous" and "ecstatic" have been used. It has been compared with the effects of music in popular love lyrics and occasionally in novels.

Few students of sex psychology have attempted an analysis here, but some keen observations have been made.

One writes that when the amorous emotion is dominant "the desire for sexual contacts often seems remote . . . One does not want dermal or genital pleasure particularly . . . One thrills at the mere presence of the beloved person and at receiving her (or his) undivided attention" (Folsom, 1934, p. 379).

Another stresses that the chief goal of this desire is the *presence* of the attractive person, though it usually prompts toward physical contact:

> It seems to consist of a continuous series of ever repeated nervous thrills which are connected if the object is near, but interrupted and arrested if the object is absent. These thrills, though exceedingly intense, do not have an organic function, but exist, as it were, for their own sake. That they are physical is obvious, and they are intensified by various physical acts, such as kissing, embracing, caressing, etc. . . . Romantic love gives free rein to all these innocent excitements and finds its full satisfaction . . . in these. (Ward, 1903, p. 400)

Comparisons with the emotional effects of music have been frequent enough to warrant treatment in a later chapter. The response in musical appreciation must be at a high level, however, to parallel the potential of amorous emotion. The likeness would hold, moreover, only for the immediate sensuous experience; it fails to convey the quality and intensity of the *developed* amorous desire that results from the *cumulative* effect of the esthetic response in falling in love. When such attraction is reinforced by valued traits of character, the mature emotion may be one of the most powerful in the human repertoire.

The phenomenon of *immediate* attraction is doubtless most familiar through the recollections of those who have directly experienced it. It is richly illustrated in fiction, especially in some of the legendary encounters of romantic literature. A wealth of biographical and autobiographical sources confirm its reality. It has been observed among the lower animals. Its occurrence under circumstances in which the expression of personality factors is absent or minimal is among the grounds for the emphasis on surface esthetics in this study of sexual attraction.

The more typical slower growth of amorous emotion will result when esthetic appeals are few in number or weak in effect. This will also be true when unattractive traits reduce the total response. Such negative elements may, of course, operate from the beginning of an association, as illustrated in the experiences of two college students. In the first example an initial strong attraction was reduced by some language habits which led to a kind of emotional rejection rather than disapproval.

This was a love affair in which I almost got engaged, and I have often wondered how it might have turned out. Annette had fine features and I thought of her as "just my type" in her general appearance. She was animated and friendly. But her family background was very different from mine. She used rather vulgar language freely and her grammar was pretty bad in spots. I tried to overlook it and concentrate on what I liked about her, but it finally changed my feelings. It was not that I looked down upon her. I'm just sensitive to things like that, especially in a girl.

In the second case an unpleasant trait is an essential part of the (physical) personality.

I met this girl at a dance, and at first I thought it was going to be an exciting evening because she certainly was easy to look at. But we had only been talking for a few minutes when I began to notice her voice. It sounded like she had a cold, sort of nasal and raspy. I soon realized it was her natural voice. It was a shame the way it spoiled the effect. It reminded me of something like that in grade school; a very pretty little girl, but her last name was so awful that it made a difference in the way I felt about her.

Sexual Differences and Amorous Attraction

Everyone knows that "character" must never be neglected in the love choice, and certainly not in the decision to marry. Virtues such as amiability, loyalty, sincerity, humor and cheerfulness are universally regarded as contributing importantly to choice and to the growth of love. Our stress on the primary role of surface features in the arousal of amorous emotion leads directly to questions as to the role of these highly valued traits. That they are important can be conceded without affecting the statement that they are not *essential* to the growth of amorous emotion.

We begin with the basic fact that for most people amorous attraction relates to the opposite sex. From this we infer that what attracts us must be something *in which men and women differ*. They differ in sex organs and in other physical features which excite the sexual impulse. They do *not* differ, as sexes, in any of the desirable traits listed above. We are, of course, "attracted" to people who exhibit any one or more of a large number of such virtues, but attraction of this kind is not amorous. We approve or "like" anyone who is kind, honest, unaffected, loyal, etc., whether male or female, and whether sexually or amorously attractive or unattractive.

For this reason the primary factors in amorous behavior must be limited to surface features. Generosity may add to the appeal of an esthetically attractive person, while selfishness will tend to reduce the overall appeal. We will be "charmed by her beauty, repelled by her character."

An apparent exception to the above statement regarding behavior differences between the sexes may now be considered. A youth gave the following account:

> I always thought of blue-eyed brunettes as my favorite type and I was attracted to this girl right away because she had black hair and very blue eyes. But there was something wrong from the beginning, although I didn't realize what it was until after I had dated her. It was in her manner. She was very direct and forceful and talked a bit too loud. She used to stare at me in a way that would make me drop my eyes like I was embarrassed, and I guess I was. She would ask me questions and say things in a kind of challenging way that put me on the defensive. I guess aggressive is the word for it. It finally began to bother me. A couple of times I met her in the company of another girl who was much quieter and maybe a little shy. She impressed me as a lot more feminine. I remember wishing the brunette was more like her. I know I'd have liked her better that way.

Are there, apart from the surface elements earlier discussed, features of behavior that directly evoke amorous emotion? Could the "feminine manner" suggested in the foregoing selection be an example of such behavior? If there are traits of this kind, we shall expect to find them, for the reasons given earlier, among those in which men and women differ as sexes.

Many such differences have been proposed as typical of what is masculine or feminine, although it is doubtful whether any one of them has ever been agreed upon as true of *all* men and women. We are concerned here, however, only with those traits active in courtship—those qualities regarded as typically masculine or feminine, which are prominent when men and women are "sexually aware" of each other.

The difference in intiative is of prime importance in the courtship setting: the male is usually the pursuer, the female the pursued. A student of the history of marriage contrasts the *active* courtship behavior of the male with the *passive* behavior of the female (Westermarck, 1925). Examples among primitives and in the animal world as well as in civilized societies have suggested that this difference may be basic to all sexual behavior (Ellis, 1936).

Must we therefore include the aggressive role of the male and the "waiting game" maneuvers of the female among the *essential* differences that make men and women attractive to each other? Is modesty and coyness in girls to be classed with beauty in attracting boys?

The facts do not support the view that this difference in behavior is universal. In the majority of the human societies surveyed in a major comparative study (Ford and Beach, 1951), it was accepted that the male *should* advance toward the female, but in practice this was often violated. Women do, on occasion, take the initiative as courters. Custom in some cultures is neutral in the matter, permitting either sex to make courting overtures; in a few others women are even expected to make the initial moves.

Among the lower animals the older view has again been found in error; courtship initiative is fairly evenly divided and is often determined by the relative strength of sexual needs. In some species the female is the more aggressive. In summary: "there is no mammalian species in which sexual initiative rests solely with either the male or the female" (Ford and Beach, 1951, p. 90).

Role differences in courtship thus vary too much to be considered as a basic of sexual behavior. They are regarded by social psychologists as a matter of custom rather than "nature." When custom prescribes that certain kinds of courtship are "right and proper," men and women will be more attractive to each other when they conform to this behavior, just as other socially approved traits will add to their appeal.

This conclusion contrasts with one concerning a more deeply rooted difference between man and woman: human beauty is of far greater sexual value to the male. Comparative studies of a large number of primitive peoples reveal that while standards of attractiveness vary greatly, "in most societies the physical beauty of the female receives more explicit consideration than does the handsomeness of the male" (Ford and Beach, 1951, p. 103). Research revealed no exceptions to this rule.

We previously quoted the observation that the love thoughts of men have always been a "perpetual meditation" on beauty. An historian, after quoting some lines of Islamic verse in praise of feminine beauty, comments that they sum up "half the poetry of the world." A student of the history of the sex relationship notes that at no time has there been, in the record of woman's emotional life, a tendency to glorify masculine beauty. The cult of human beauty-worship is exclusively male (Lucka, 1915).

Differences between the sexes are rarely if ever absolute. It may be doubted that women in any society are entirely indifferent to the esthetic attractions of the male, however much they tend—as is often said of primitives—to place greater value on strength and valor. No one need be told that in our own culture the feminine response to the male is not without esthetic interest. The fact that women are culturally conditioned to be more restrained in their sexual responsiveness must have operated to obscure or reduce the expression of feelings of attraction. But although the difference is one of degree and is partly of cultural origin, that it does exist appears to be beyond question, and we may say that sexual love, as a response to esthetic values, appears not to be the same experience for women as for men.*

The structures of the sex organs have been seen as physical symbols of the difference in roles between man and woman: one to "advance and penetrate," the other to receive; the male part active, the female passive. The difference in emotional experience may be compared with that of the physical behavior. The male is pursuer because he is charmed; the female is pursued because she exhibits the charm; she desires pursuit because she is gratified in receiving admiration. The male is active in the desire to possess this esthetically pleasing person, and is gratified when conquest is achieved. The female's role is passive in that she enjoys being sought, and sought because admired and valued. The difference, then, is between the experience of desiring to possess what is attractive and the experience, of *being* attractive, and finally of granting possession.

Exaggerated expressions of a motive can sometimes define it most clearly. A woman who was admittedly a "philanderess" provided a rather vivid description of the subjective side of one element of the "essential feminine."

* Theodor Reik writes: "Schools now teach boys and girls anatomy and biology, but no one teaches them that the psychology of the sexes is different . . . that love does not mean the same thing to men and women, that sexuality has a different meaning for the sexes, that it has a different emotional place in their lives. More than thirty-seven years of psycho-analytic practice have shown me how much unhappiness between men and women is due to lack of understanding . . . of the relationships of the sexes" (Reik, 1964, p. 97).

Some people think I'm vain and perhaps I am, but I think every woman is like me at heart because I know every woman enjoys being attractive. I'll admit I enjoy it more than anything else in life. I love to have men look at me and want me. It's more important that they look at my face than at my figure, but I enjoy both. I enjoy being admired by women almost as much as by men, but of course the important difference is that men *want* me. I mean they want to date me and of course they want all they can get. But I enjoy being looked at by almost anybody, even an unattractive man.

Dressing is very important to me and I love beautiful colors and patterns, but most of all I think of how people will react to what I wear. I like quiet clothing, in good taste, but I never want my clothes to get more attention than *I* do.

I read quite a lot, especially the news magazines for current events and activities. I'm really interested in these things and I enjoy reading. But I'll admit it's partly so I can tell about what I read. I'd hate to have anybody look at me and think I'm attractive but not very bright, or that my personality is sort of empty.

I enjoy sex, of course, but apart from the pleasure I enjoy being sexually exciting and knowing a man desires me. I guess I'm quite an exhibitionist. I love to expose my body to a man I'm fond of and when the relationship is right. I mean when I know him well enough and really want him.

Maybe I'll marry some day but I can't endure the thought that my husband would come to take me for granted and not look at me any more the way men do now. The best part of life, to me, is to enjoy being attractive at least part of every day, especially in the evening, after work. I like to have a date about every other night, at least. I like to go to public places where there are a lot of people, like big bars and dining rooms and hotels.

Sometimes, when I see very plain girls, I wonder what their lives must be like. I know that there are a lot of other things in life that are interesting and important. They are important to me too. It's just that the real cream of living is being an exciting person to be with because I'm attractive.*

Many would regard such a person as immature and shallow, and would ask does she not want to be valued for character and "personality"? Is she really content with admiration for her face, figure and clothing?

It is our premise that *sexual* attraction between man and woman must be defined in terms of sex differences. These, for the male, are traits and qualities that are physically and mentally feminine, and if we exclude for the moment the genital-sexual factor, the limit must be set at what is *esthetically* feminine. However narrow such a statement of woman's esthetic sexuality may seem, it is rooted in the core, above the genital level, of her sexual value for the male. The distinctively feminine element in her own courtship experience is the pleasure of what may be seen as *normal narcissism.* In whatever other ways she may attract, as by her interests, amiability, animation, humor, she will be valued as a *person* rather than as a member of her sex. It may

* The sexual orientation seen in this document is, of course, highly unusual and the "philosophy" expressed would doubtless be rejected by an increasing number of women as reflecting an excessive development of the traditional role of the female in our society. The case is offered only to illustrate a component of feminine psychology which may operate more moderately as one element of the "essential feminine" in many or most women, and which may be deeper in source than the social settings that may affect it positively or negatively from one culture to another. In this instance the individual gave every appearance of being a spontaneous and whole-hearted narcissist who would have been similarly motivated in any time or place.

hardly be necessary to add that her appeal and meaning as a person is a vital part of what makes her attractive as a *companion*. Without this she will have little to offer during those many periods in any association when the sexual value of a partner is secondary.

Art and Sex Esthetics

Students of art make a basic distinction between *form* and *content*. The content of a picture is what it is about, that is, its subject, theme or story; thus, nature, a dramatic event, or a human likeness. Form refers to the way the artist has used line and color and has organized the parts into a pattern. When, in viewing a picture, we are conscious of visual pleasure apart from the subject, we are responding to form. When we are interested mainly in the meaning, as tragic or inspiring, historical or erotic, we are responding to content.

Form is best illustrated when content is least emphasized, when the lines and colors are not intended to convey meaning, but to elicit pleasure in the patterns themselves, as in much modern abstract art. In music the same distinction applies. The composer may intend to convey such "content" as gaiety, sadness, serenity, majesty, and so on. He may, on the other hand, offer no more than sheer figures of notes, pure sound-pleasure, without intended meanings, without trying to tell a story.

The *surface* traits discussed earlier may be said to correspond to the form element in art and music. The total impression may be highly complex despite the apparent simplicity of the elements. Traits that contribute to the esthetic impression a person conveys include, for example, the several profiles of the head and the degree of moulding of the features; the tint and texture of the skin; the spacing of the eyes, the size and curvature of the mouth, the prominence and angle of the chin; the color of the eyes; the color, texture and coiffure of the hair; the proportions of the body and the characteristics of body movement.

To these elements may be added a curious and striking phenomenon of perception itself; a quality of expression may arise through the effect of the different features upon each other. The impression of a face is more than the sum of its features. A change in the contour of the chin, for example, may reduce or increase the attractiveness of the upper part of the face. Part and whole influence each other.

Our thesis with regard to sex-esthetic attraction is simply that its basis is the structure and pattern, line and movement, tone and color, which correspond to the form element in art, and that it is the perception of these, along with individual qualities of style and mannerism, that arouses amorous emotion when the perceiver encounters the *combination* to which he is most responsive.

What, finally, corresponds to *content* in sexual esthetics? One way to state it would be: all *else* about behavior—everything that cannot be classed as form. It includes everything a person is and does apart from whatever is attractive or unattractive about the way he does it, or from whatever is pleasing to the eye and ear in his manner or style.* When we consider a person's interests or opinions, or his socially approved or disapproved traits of personality, we are responding to him in this sense.

---

*One example of the meaning of personal style is furnished by a girl who observed: "This man had a kind of pride or dignity I greatly admired. He would never do anything awkward or even slightly humiliating, as a matter of principle, or so it seemed to me. He would not ask a favor no matter what could be gained by it. It was a kind of poise or standard he had deep

Writers on art have described the response to pictorial beauty as "purely contemplative," meaning that appreciation is an end in itself. It does not prompt to further action; the enjoyment is a completed experience.

Beyond question there is contemplative pleasure of this kind in the association of the sexes. The case of the sexual esthete who followed women to enjoy visually the grace of their walking movements is a fair example. Much more commonly the face, voice, manner and style are the center of attention in a variety of social settings in which response is limited to perceptual pleasure alone.

If pleasure in art is always and solely contemplative, however, it is obvious that the sex-esthetic response is often a quite different experience. Amorous attraction usually includes, in addition to visual pleasure, the impulse to approach and eventually to make some kind and degree of contact. Observations of children have revealed that beauty is a factor in the early expression of attraction, with interest shown in moving closer, sitting together, touching, holding hands, and finally in some form of embrace. Amorous attraction at all ages culminates in physical contact.

Artistic and sexual appreciation do have in common the desire to possess, so far as possible, the source of pleasure.

---

inside. I mean it wouldn't matter whether anyone was looking. It was part him, and I thought it was sort of heroic, in a way. I think it was an important part of what made him attractive to me."

Another example from Plutarch, concerning Cleopatra: "Her actual beauty was not in itself so remarkable that none could be compared with her, or that no one could see her without being struck by it, but the contact of her presence, if you lived with her, was irresistible. The attraction of her person, joining with the charm of her conversation, and the character that attended all she said or did, was something bewitching." (Quoted in S. Hook, *The Hero in History* [Boston: Beacon Press, 1955], p. 177)

As one of many possible illustrations, the connoisseur of feminine walking movements acknowledged an urge, sometimes painfully frustrated when he encountered an unusually charming specimen, "to somehow own her, have her belong to me so that I could enjoy her whenever I wanted to."

That there is some kind of linkage between sexual and general esthetics has seemed probable to a number of students. Something was needed in animal evolution to bring the sexes together from a distance—visible details that would draw them into contacts that would then prompt to further responses. George Santayana, one of the few writers on esthetics to define its relationship to sex, believes that our entire esthetic sensibility is traceable to the sexual impulse, that responsiveness to sexual beauty is the source of appreciation of all beauty. Our emotional life would have been very different, he thinks, had nature somehow solved the reproduction problem without sex. But nature failed to restrict the esthetic sense to sex alone, and the response to nonsexual beauty may be seen as a marginal and less vigorous outgrowth or radiation of the original: "the whole sentimental side of our aesthetic sensibility— without which it would be perceptive and mathematical rather than aesthetic—is due to our sexual organization remotely stirred" (Santayana, 1896, p. 44). Schopenhauer long ago observed that "no object transports us so quickly into pure aesthetic contemplation as the most beautiful human countenance and form." Sex esthetics may be the original source of every art form.

Sex-esthetic Perception

Descriptions of certain of the facets of human esthetic attraction as an experience may be difficult. There are qualities in the configurations of the facial features, in the voice and in the movements of the body that are literally inexpressible, yet they are among the basics of amorous emotion. A few years ago an advertiser, to catch attention, printed a number of photographs of cinema celebrities paired with those of persons regarded as near-duplicates in resemblance. Feature by feature these pairs were often remarkably similar, yet the differences in overall impression were usually at once apparent. The distinguishing elements, however, were very difficult to define.

In a photographic likeness there are features which may be named or specified by adjectives, but the total effect of their combination may be impossible to put into words. Apart from this there can be no one-to-one correspondence between the details of a photograph and the elements of language, as Suzanne Langer has pointed out. "For this reason the correspondence between a word-picture and a visible object can never be as close as that between the object and its photograph" (Langer, 1948, p. 77). Her statement that a photograph or a painting "has no vocabulary" is emphatically true of esthetic appreciation of the human face, especially when attraction is sharply focused on what for the observer is some unique charm of line, contour, or expressive detail.

Experiences of this kind cannot easily be put into words, and so cannot be conveyed to others. Amorous emotion develops, of course, not from perceptions but from the feelings aroused by perceptions. Feelings, however, are often notoriously difficult to describe. Is there a *way* of expressing the feelings associated with esthetic forms or patterns?

The medium best adapted to this purpose, Langer has proposed, is music. "That musical structures . . . resemble certain dynamic patterns of human experience is a well-established fact. . . . the real power of music lies in the fact that it can be 'true' to the life of feeling in a way that language cannot . . ." (pp. 183, 197). Music can express certain feelings with greater fidelity than words because there is a correspondence between musical forms and the "forms" of the emotional life. There may be experiences for which one art is more expressive than another; it "may well be . . . that erotic emotions are most readily formulated in musical terms" (p. 209). The countless popular songs that combine melody with amorous lyrics provide one kind of illustration, and the thesis is sometimes explicit; e.g., "a pretty girl is like a melody."

A further parallel between attraction and music is that sexual allure, to be most intriguing, needs a touch of something suggested but not defined. A musical theme may similarly lack fixed meaning; it may be open to many interpretations. It is expressive but asserts nothing, or its meaning is not completed.

The qualities of music may closely resemble emotional states in that the sound may best express the *mood* of the emotion. Music, according to one view, was for a long while identified with the voice, in song; gradually it became separated from the lyric and appreciated for itself alone, though its origins are still reflected in program music. Its more abstract forms, detached from any content, drew further away from its source than those of any other art. It is this abstract music that most closely parallels to the "esthetic surface" in sexual attraction—the sheer molding and spacing of the features, the line of the profile, the coloring and texture of the skin, the pitch and timbre of the voice.

Esthetic theory offers little, however, to help us understand the experience of sexual beauty. Concerning abstract music it has been stated:

An analysis of these perceptions could only be undertaken on the basis of a theory of musical esthetics, and no satisfactory theory exists. No theory has yet been proposed, such as Darwin's theory that music is a highly developed form of the sexual calls of animals . . . that gives any explanation of why one musical phrase is pleasing and another not, nor, more important still, why one sequence of phrases seems satisfactory, stimulating and "logical" while another sequence appears arbitrary and boring. (Sullivan, 1937, p. 51)

The response to sexual beauty has been seen as the most fundamental as well as the most common human esthetic experience—the one appreciation in this mode of which almost everyone is capable. The "man in the street" may not be moved by masterpieces of painting or sculpture, but he is sure he knows an attractive female when he sees one, and usually responds emotionally to his perception.

To some students these perceptions have seemed related, at a deep level, to those of the artist, whose sensibilities are merely more highly developed or specialized for other fields of natural objects. When a van Gogh says of a landscape: "I cannot tell you often enough, I am ravished, ravished with what I see . . . ," he is reacting to visual patterns of line and color with emotion which seems closely comparable to that of the sexual esthetes described in some of our earlier illustrations. The language of the artist may often be suggestively similar to that of a person sharply smitten by love at first sight.

While the emotions and impulses of the artist and the lover obviously differ in certain ways, they have one important feature in common: the desire to *fix* and preserve, on canvas with paint, seems in kinship with the desire to *possess* another, which is the core of the amorous emotion. Beyond the moment of the experience itself, nothing remains in either case but to perpetuate it, to have it as often and as long as possible.

Why should there be two different kinds of human sexuality and why should attraction occur at an age far too early for the reproductive purpose of sex?

The last question could, of course, be asked regarding the sexual impulse itself. The capacity of the male infant for erection and erotic excitation seems quite pointless in the context of biology. Propagation of the species is of such vast importance, it would seem, that nature begins sexual development long before it will be called upon to function. (Such prematurity has been suggested as comparable to a very early arrival for an appointment, prompted by its vital importance). In its fully matured form the amorous-esthetic response may be seen as a means of ensuring the cohabitation of male and female for a long enough time to guarantee by repeated sexual activity the fertilization of the ovum and perhaps to compensate for the periodic loss of interest of the sexually satiated animal.

In a larger view, another issue is raised. *Natural selection,* as the basic formula for evolution, centers upon the utility of all human and animal functions. Sexual love, in this light, keeps the mating pair together not only to increase the probability of fertilization but to secure protection of the offspring through double parental care. Is the romantic experience no more, then, than a device serving as a marginal aid to reproduction? The question is one of several of the same kind: that of the sheer biological value, for example, of the esthetic sense in its broader and nonsexual meanings. Our responsiveness to the many beautiful things in nature has every appearance of being an end in itself rather than a means to an end. Male fascination with female charms, *as an experience,* moreover, clearly extends beyond its utilitarian function. While it may well be an aid to reproduction and survival, it is also quite definitely in a class with several other human functions which appear to have developed far beyond the range of the natural selection formula. Among these are the appreciation of all art forms which are completely free of sexual connotation. They include such diverse capacities as man's self-awareness, his imagination, his sense of humor and ability to laugh; likewise, some would say, his "religious" sense of wonder and awe in contemplating the universe. These human attributes seem to be bonuses rather than practical tools; luxuries rather than necessities.

The role of individuality is surely a large one in any effort to define the romantic experience, not only because its value for the individual may be quite different from its value for the species, but also because for some romance is far more meaningful than for others. For primitive man, or for the peasant—the "man with the hoe"—it must mean far less than for a Dante, a Goethe, or for the amorous devotee of *Manon Lescaut.* When the romantic experience can profoundly shape the course of a person's life it may be a challenge to biology as well as to psychology. In this view the amorous-esthetic component of sexuality takes its place among other functions at the higher levels of human capacity with comparable meaning for the issue of the purposiveness of "creative evolution." The reason why we fall in love may thus be linked with the reason why we became more complex than the lower animals, or why we became human.

CHAPTER 5

The Varieties of Esthetic Attraction

Attraction, as earlier noted, always involves selection, even among young children and some of the lower animals. Unrelated persons are never identical in appearance, and choice is nearly always possible between any two or more individuals. Almost everyone is attractive to someone, and is eventually selected as a mate.

Sexual attractiveness has many meanings and is rated according to diverse standards. Two very different physical types may both be regarded as "attractive," and, among a number of individuals with excellent features—for example, the participants in a beauty contest—most people could readily choose one that they found more beautiful than the others. Beauty and attractiveness are definitely not the same, and "even a high degree of beauty may have a low degree of attractiveness." (Ellis, 1936, I, 3:191).

Surface features may seem of small weight in attraction, since our tradition regarding sexual love, especially when it leads to marriage, tends to stress much more vital traits of character, disposition, and temperament. It is our thesis, nevertheless, that *it is among these esthetically perceived structures and characteristics* that the basic sources of the amorous emotion are to be found. It is here that, as an

87

eminent psychologist phrased it long ago, we may read "the alphabet . . . of which romantic love is so largely composed, where trivial often eclipse great qualities, and one trait may be magnified beyond all bounds" (Hall, 1904, II: 114–15).

What is considered beautiful may vary greatly from one society to another, from which some observers have concluded that attractiveness is entirely a matter of custom and fashion, that preferences are shaped largely by what happens to be the mode in a given culture and period of history. Fashion, a sociologist wrote, "determines what type of female beauty is at any time preferred—plump or svelte, blonde or brunette, large or petite, red-haired or black-haired" (Sumner, 1906, p. 191). In studies of this kind on primitive peoples, the differences revealed are at times more impressive than the similarities. Traits of highest interest may vary from group to group. One society favors a slender figure, another a much heavier one; sometimes small eyes are preferred, sometimes large ones.

There are definite trends of similarity. The Trobriand Islanders for example, are most attentive, as we are, to the eyes, mouth, nose, and hair; voice quality and grace of movement are also important. They differ in their preference for small eyes and heavy lips, shaved eyebrows and, of course, a brown skin. That there are common elements is illustrated by the admiration that individuals of one racial group may have for those of a widely different one; for example, the modern European male may find attractive women among primitive societies. Another observer was impressed, however by "the endless personal variations which may all be said to come within the limits of possible beauty or charm . . . Among the multitude of minute differences . . . the beholder is variously attracted and repelled according to his own individual idiosyncrasy" (Ellis, 1936, I, 3:184).

The core of the problem of sexual choice is the fact that within a given society, whatever its standards, there will be a variety of individual preferences. These preferences, moreover, tend definitely to center on certain parts. An investigator of a culture in India, for example, noted that the people judged attractiveness feature by feature rather than as a whole. (Elwin, 1939). The finding has often been repeated and appears to be generally true; it is important because it means that attraction is a phenomenon that can be *analyzed.* It ranges from features which are quite commonly agreed upon as of primary interest to nearly everyone, to others which are progressively of less and less interest to the majority, and finally to some which rarely attract the attention of most people but which are of high value for a few. At one end of the scale we will expect to find the eyes, hair, facial profile, voice, hands; at the other end we will find the contour of the hairline, the size and shape of the ears, the carriage and movements of the body in walking. One woman, for example, commented: "The back of a man's neck excites me. I don't have a mania about it but I like a well-formed . . . neck. The back of a man's neck is the first thing I look at" (Henry, 1941, I:250). One of the writer's subjects said, "I won't say it's really the most important thing but I always notice the front contour of a girl's jaw line. I like a tapering face with a small narrow chin. I could never fall for a girl with a broad or square front profile. It's not that it means anything about her personality. It's just that I don't like the lines." The slope of the shoulders, the arching of the brows, the shape and modelling of the nose, the pitch of the voice and the mode or style of laughter have all been included among the findings of studies of this kind. Some studies have revealed sex differences in the "analytical" type of response. One investigator (Hamilton, 1929) asked 200 persons whether they responded to a "particular type" of person of the opposite sex. The males of the group named 109 characteristics, with only 13 failing to specify any preference. About half of the women, on the other hand, expressed no feelings about attractive traits.

Fetishisms

A rich source of illustrations, as well as an important field of evidence, is available among the peculiar forms of human sexuality known as fetishisms. The characteristics of these reactions in many instances so closely resemble those of the familiar amorous emotional state, both in sensual and esthetics aspects, as to suggest to a number of students that the key to normal sexual love may lie in these abnormal sexual phenomena.

In many fetishisms the unusual feature lies simply in the extraordinary value of a specific part of the body or of a facet of behavior. Some of these are well within the range of normal sexual interest. Feminine hair, for example, entices most men, but for the hair fetishist it may be so outstanding a lure as to reduce all else to minor concern, so that he can truthfully say "the girl herself matters little if her hair is attractive. Nothing else about her is of interest to me."

In our society the feminine leg, needless to say, is a stimulus to the male, doubtless in part as a token of the figure as a whole, but certainly also as an object of admiration and an erotic value in itself. Few men, however, would be likely to rate the leg as more important than the facial features. For the leg *fetishist* these values may be reversed. His interest in other parts of the body may vary, but he will concentrate first and foremost on the legs. For one of these "leg men," studied by the writer, a shapely leg, clad in nylon and with the foot encased in a stylish high-heeled shoe, was by far the most exciting erotic and esthetically arousing spectacle he could imagine. At rest to some degree, but especially in motion, it was almost the sole focus of attention.

While sensual excitement was in this case primary there was also clear evidence of esthetic appreciation. The subject had well-defined standards regarding the profile and especially the "taper" of his preferred type of leg, also as to the kind of shoe required for harmony. He might be quite disappointed and frustrated at sight of a shapely leg in the wrong style of footwear, for example a flat heel, or too much ornamentation. These affected him, he remarked, "the way a combination of a beautiful face and bow-legs would affect the average man." He used terms in describing the fetish, such as "delicacy," "daintiness," and "lovliness" which were much more suggestive of an esthetic response than of sensual arousal. On encountering a woman whose legs and shoes more or less met his requirements he might follow her about for a considerable time. He reported that despite his basic timidity in approaching women he could be quite daring in efforts to become acquainted with such a person.

The human hand, again using our own society as a standard, is among the more minor items of attraction and is more often of esthetic than of erotic interest, yet the hand fetishist is by no means unknown. Reported cases may be quite closely compared with the leg-and-shoe enthusiast in that for both, the fetish object is simply the outstanding point of attraction and that for each a part of the body normally of minor interest becomes foremost. One fetishist of the feminine hand is described as notably interested in hands well before sexual maturity, the erotic response to a beautiful hand developing gradually. In his encounters with women the hand was the center of attention and he was sensitive to all of the details of an attractive one. He was not, however—and this in parallel with more normal sexuality—interested in those of aged persons, or of the very young, and he did not respond to the male hand, however well formed.

Apart from this exceptional interest in what for most would be secondary, the behavior of the fetishist often resembles that of a person in the throes of a romantically amorous state. The obsessive preoccupation, the often powerful desire to *possess* the attractive object, may be very much like that of the normal lover. A number of students of sex psychology have been struck by this likeness and by the question it raises; could it be that the sexually or romantically fixated person differs from the fetishist mainly in the peculiarly specialized or eccentric character of the latter's interest? Is the romantic attraction simply a fetishism common to many, and fetishism itself only an *uncommon* kind of attraction?

The great French psychologist Alfred Binet, a systematic observer of human sexual behavior, was the first to see a link between the normal and the abnormal kinds of attraction, or between what he regarded as *major* and *minor* fetishisms (Binet, 1887). He proposed that normal attraction could be understood in terms of its similarity to fetishism. *We are all fetishists,* he suggested, so far as amorous desire tends to focus upon any one or more specific traits of a person whom we find attractive. He was much impressed with the intermediate cases of fetishism, since he saw them as the bridge to normal choice. In the ordinary kinds of preference with which we are all familiar were the germs of the extreme cases. There are minor fetishisms all around us if we could recognize them, and here we may find an explanation of the occasional extraordinary attractions and puzzling marriages in which, for example, a person with many assets is apparently mismated with someone quite lacking in merits.

The kind of attraction Binet had in mind is well illustrated in an episode in the amorous life of James II of England, as described by Macaulay:

> The beauty . . . which distinguished the favorite ladies of Charles was not necessary to James. . . . when young, [he] had surrendered his liberty, descended below his rank and incurred the displeasure of his family, for the coarse features of Anne Hyde. He had soon, to the great diversion of the whole court, been drawn away from his plain consort by a plainer mistress, Arabella Churchill. . . . But of all his illicit attachments the strongest was that which bound him to Catharine Sedley . . . Personal charm she had none, with the exception of two brilliant eyes, the lustre of which, to men of delicate taste, seemed fierce and unfeminine. Her form was lean, her countenance haggard. Charles, though he liked her conversation, laughed at her ugliness, and said that the priests must have recommended her to his brother by way of penance. . . . Catharine herself was astonished by the violence of his passion. "It cannot be my beauty," she said, "for he must see that I have none; and it cannot be my wit; for he has not enough to know that I have any." (Macaulay, n.d., pp. 52–54)

Binet saw clearly that fetishism is much more than a genital-sex reaction: "for fetishists the sense perception of the loved object is a source of pleasure superior even to sexual sensation." What he refers to as the "sense perception" is the esthetic response in attraction; it is the "pursuit of beauty," he states, as an end in itself, and quite apart from sensual pleasure. There is an *esthetic fetishism* which may be of greater value than the erotic experience.

Sexual *beauty*, Binet emphasizes, is a word with many meanings; or rather, it has a different meaning for each person, since the variety of individual tastes and preferences is endless. Fetishism is the outstanding symbol of this variety; it represents the furthest reaches of individuality in sexual choice. Amorous emotion is in essence the "adoration and pursuit" of beauty as each individual defines it. Following Binet a number of others have accepted and stressed the idea of many grades or degrees between fetishism and normal choice, or between major and minor fetishisms (Ellis, 1936; Hirschfeld, 1935; Kahn, 1931; Kraft-Ebing, 1908). The fetishist who is relatively indifferent to all else about a person who bears the trait that charms him is seen as closely related to the lover so entranced with the unique beauty of his chosen one that he is quite willing to overlook serious flaws, or is perhaps merely unable to see them.

The view that certain mental deviations differ only in degree from normality is a familiar principle in abnormal psychology. William James, the great American psychologist, once stated it in a manner well fitted to the present context.

> the elementary mechanisms of our life are presumably so uniform that what is shown to be true in a marked degree of some persons is probably true in some degree of all, and may in a few be true in an extraordinarily high degree. . . . phenomena are best understood when placed within their series, studied in their germ . . . and compared with their exaggerated kindred. (James, 1963, p. 382)

If sexual love is an emotion aroused by certain esthetic responses, and if fetishisms are essentially extremes of the same process, there should be evidence in the experiences of the fetishist. Often the accounts of these experiences, with their emphasis on their obsessive and rapturous character, are strongly suggestive of the presence of something more than erotic excitement. The language may be quite familiar in its likeness to that of the normal expressions of amorous emotion, differing only in the object that arouses it. Thus: "I have an unbounded passion for beautiful, slim, well-formed hands. . . . I have an unconquerable desire to caress such hands" (Hirschfeld, 1932, p. 86). Another, after stealing a lock of hair, states: ". . . I go home and kiss the charming hair again and again, I press it to my nose and cheeks and breathe in the precious fragrance of it" (Hirschfeld, 1932, p. 67). A teen-age fetishist of feminine hair, questioned closely as to what the object meant to him, could say only that he experienced pleasure in combing it, without marks of any sexual excitement; he was interested, however, only in the hair of the opposite sex (Moll, 1898).

Clear evidence of amorous-esthetic response in the experience of fetishism appears in a case thoroughly studied by the writer. The subject is an articulate man with an analytical attitude toward his sexual experiences.

The emotion I feel on encountering a woman of refined and distinguished appearance wearing shoes of delicate or dainty construction is particularly arresting and exciting. This emotion *is not exclusively one of sexual excitement.* The charm of the shoes, shapely ankles and legs imparts an alluring effect to her whole person. The feeling I then have about her is *very similar to that of being "in love,"* or at least to the beginning of this state. This feeling centers, however, on her shoes, legs and ankles, and I have experienced a stronger urge to kiss or caress such a woman's lower extremities than to kiss her lips, unless she is exceptionally beautiful. If she should remove her shoes, she immediately loses much of her magnetic quality. I have vividly experienced this kind of loss of interest on several occasions. The type of person who wears the shoes is very important. Handsome shoes on an immature and frivolous sort of girl have a much less pronounced effect upon me.

At such encounters the subject becomes strongly excited sexually and under favorable conditions is able to reach climax. He reports greater awareness of the esthetic elements of the fetish, as well as of the personality as a whole, after sexual excitement subsides.

This man recalls nonsexual interest in feminine shoes, especially those of slipper style and with high heels, dating from the elementary school period; he reports the development of erotic excitement with fantasies of shoes accompanying masturbation during these years. Interest somewhat later included the form of the leg, but did not extend above the knee. "In addition I needed shapely ankles and sheer hose, preferably the darker shades. The effect was much increased by movements of the foot. No part of the leg above the knee held any interest for me."

An important feature of the case is the subject's quite normal capacity for love relationships, clearly evident in an intense attachment during a period in which fetish interest was in an inactive phase. He is thus able to testify to the presence of an emotion in the fetish experience which is easily distinguishable from the erotic effect and identical in quality to that of normal sexual love, the sole difference being that it is associated with fetish rather than with the whole person.

A case which may be classed as intermediate between those preceding and those to follow may be included here as an illustration of the linkage between the major and minor forms. This "sexual esthete" is a professional man in his early fifties.

> According to your writings on fetishism I would have to call myself one if it's just a matter of degree. I am very strongly moved by the lines of a woman's trunk, with special reference to the contour of the hips and buttocks. If these lines are right, and if she

carries herself with grace, I can say that I think there are few things more beautiful on earth. If such a woman were my wife I could hardly ask much more than that she walk about in an undergarment or a bathing suit. I would be in ecstasy and I think I would never tire. I can only compare the effect with that of some of my favorite phrases and themes in music, chiefly in Beethoven, Brahms and Mozart. There is one theme in Brahms, especially, that "says" it perfectly.

I have followed women on the street for blocks when the lines and movements were just right. It's emotional rather than physical, but it is sexual too, because men don't affect me that way to nearly the same degree.

I react like any other man to breasts and legs, but when it comes to sex in the usual sense I prefer a different figure from what I have described, a fuller and more voluptuous body.

Minor and Normal Fetishisms: Literary Examples

Robert Burton wrote, centuries ago: "Not one in a thousand falls in love, but there is some peculiar part or other which pleaseth most, and inflames him above the rest" (Burton, 1859, III:57). The nonscientific observer, and especially the novelist, has often been more perceptive than the psychologist in this region of the emotional life.*

* No apology is offered for the use of literary illustrations. Many psychologists will agree with the observation that "novelists, poets, and playwrights have had deeper insights into human nature than we have yet been able to bring into the laboratory is a truth of which, in this age of psychoanalysis, no one needs to be reminded . . ." (A. Kaplan, *The New World of Philosophy* [New York: Random House, 1961] p. 113). The comment by the same

Here one of the latter expresses very well the "analytic" view of attraction which is one of the main themes of this book.

No doubt, for each individual, there existed in one other mortal some physical detail which he or she could find only in this particular person. It might be the veriest trifle. Some found it, it seemed, in the colour of an eye; some in the modulations of a voice, the curve of a lip, the shape of a hand, the lines of a body in motion. Whatever it chanced to be, it was most often an insignificant characteristic, which for others did not exist, but which, to the one affected by it, made instant appeal . . . (Richardson, 1930, pp. 549–50).

In the widely acclaimed novel *Lolita,* Vladimir Nabokov has supplied a clear, accurate, and memorable account of the experience of esthetic fetishism in the form of a special sensitivity to certain physical features of feminine adolescence. For the central character—a fetishist by our definition—there are qualities in the undeveloped female body which he finds, in certain girls, extremely charming, and in one outstanding instance the supreme esthetic experience of his life. It is also very definitely a *love* fixation of the full-blown romantic type.

This fetishist responds to the immature body of the twelve-year-old Lolita; her "lovely gentle bones . . . the smooth, downward-tapering back," are *for him* supremely beautiful. Compared to the pleasures of caressing such a creature there is "no other bliss on earth." He is strongly affected by her movements, ravished by the way she walks, and especially by her graceful gyrations as she plays tennis.

---

writer that "professors of psychology" may need such reminders is unnecessary . Copious citations from literary sources may be found in professional writings, especially from Shakespeare, Dostoevsky, and the classical Greek dramatists.

His esthetic response to her postures at certain moments is exceedingly intense. She "had a way of raising her bent left knee at the ample and springy start of the service cycle when there would develop and hang in the sun for a second a vital web of balance between toed foot, pristine armpit, burnished arm and far back-flung racket . . ." (Nabokov, 1966, p. 211). For him these momentary figures of motion are inexpressibly enchanting, and he agonizes, at a later period, that he did not preserve them on film.

The effect of these charms includes the erotic, for Lolita's lover can almost reach climax, at times, by watching her. But to a greater extent the effect is amorous—it is a "love at first sight" and it is enduring; he adores "every pore and follicle of her pubescent body." In retrospect, having finally lost her, he knows "as clearly as I know I am to die, that I loved her more than anything I had ever seen or imagined on earth, or hoped for anywhere else."

Lolita illustrates several important features of our thesis of amorous emotion. First, what made this novel outstanding is the skill of its description of an amorous-esthetic experience of remarkable depth and intensity. The erotic references are only occasional and marginal; the lover's greatest joy lies in *contemplation;* it is esthetic appreciation that gives her beauty by far its highest value. In a later phase of the relationship there is much tenderness and solicitude, and the strength of the bond shows clearly in the fact that it survives a partial loss—as the girl matures—of the traits that gave it birth.

It is quite apparent that the emotion is aroused by *surface* traits; it is the physical structures and distinctive molding of the adolescent body and the characteristics of its movements that makes the essence of the enchantment. The girl's personality is as immature and shallow as that of most members of her age group, with little that could be mentally stimulating to a mature adult. Her smile is radiant and endearing, but lacking in depth or meaning. A few mannerisms or "ways" are appealing, but it is on the whole despite rather than because of any traits of personality that the powerful emotion develops.

Finally, the account may be said to describe a *major* fetishism in that an intense attraction is aroused by aspects of structure and behavior which may fairly safely be said to be sexually and esthetically stimulating for few mature adults, and which for many might well be neutral in effect or even unesthetic. The emotional state described, however, is recognizably the same in quality as that of any strong romantic attraction of the more common varieties. It is *what* this fetishist reacts to, rather than the *way* he reacts, that makes him different.

The central theme of Thomas Mann's highly acclaimed novella *Death in Venice* provides another illustration of amorous emotion based exclusively on esthetic surface traits. It describes the encounter of an aging man with a boy of fourteen.

The attraction is almost entirely visual, with occasional references to the boy's voice. It is one-sided and without communication; the lover and the beloved do not speak. Description of the boy is wholly physical. We know only that he is strikingly beautiful, that his features are flawless, his skin like ivory, his hair ringletted and of a "golden darkness." His eyes are a "strange, twilit grey." His manner and movements are uniquely charming and graceful.

Of the boy's personality we are told nothing, yet the lover, in a matter of days, becomes thoroughly fascinated. Much of the story is devoted to his transports of admiration as he watches the boy at play. He is truly enamored, completely preoccupied, knows "that he could not exist were the lad to pass from his sight."

The attraction is explicitly an *infatuation;* it is "absurd, abject . . . yet sacred too." It is, in short, amorous emotion in its purest form, unalloyed with any response to traits of character or disposition. There is no hint of genital sexuality, though there are several references to the idealized and romantic pederasty of the classical Greeks. The age difference, moreover, is great enough to make unlikely any degree of interest at an intellectual level.

One of Bernard Malamud's short stories, "The Magic Barrel," supplies an unusually vivid example of esthetic fetishism. Leo Finkle is in search of a wife, with the help of a marriage broker. Several disappointments are described; the broker is becoming discouraged. Then, as Finkle is looking through a collection of photographs of marriage-minded ladies, he comes upon a small one, of poor quality. "He gazed at it a moment and let out a cry."

To the small cheap photo he responds deeply, with great emotion. The face is "hauntingly familiar, yet absolutely strange." The girl is not exceptionally beautiful but there is something indefinable in the expression of her eyes. He reads various possibilities into the expression; his excitement continues. With a sense of great urgency he knows that he must find her. Filled with emotion he seeks the marriage broker. The latter responds with shock, for the photo, included with the rest by accident, is that of his own daughter, who is wild, shameful, utterly rejected by her parents. Her father makes it clear that she is fit for no one as a mate.

Finkle recovers from this quickly, however, and continues to be haunted by the image. "Through days of torment he struggled endlessly not to love her . . ." If she is evil, he must try to save her, but it would be to save her for himself, for he realizes now that he is committed. He has literally fallen in love with a photograph.

It is notable that the subject, or victim, of this passion

reacts ("gives a cry") the moment he sees the photo. Since he knows nothing whatever about the girl it is obvious that he must be responding solely to an impression of the features and what they convey. It is the eyes that move him so greatly, "touch his heart"; there is something strange about them; he sees suffering, regret, "whole realms of possibility." There is no hesitation; desire is immediate, brought about by *expression,* an esthetic factor that plays an important role in attraction.

Expression rather than esthetic structure is the center of an amorous fixation described by Ivan Turgenev in his novel *Fathers and Sons.* The Princess R. is "strikingly well made . . . yet no one would have called her a beauty." Her eyes are her salient feature, not their structure but their expression, which is "carefree to the verge of bravado and pensive to the verge of dejection; an enigmatic look." The character Kirsanov falls in love with her quickly and passionately, and soon achieves a conquest which includes physical surrender. His success does not, however, diminish his ardor. Despite the ease of his triumph, he becomes even more strongly fixated, for there is something "hallowed and inaccessible" about this woman. "It seemed as if she were under the sway of certain mysterious forces which were beyond even her own ken; they played with her as they willed . . ."

In intellect she is not impressive, and she is a creature of mood and impulse. There are symptoms, never clearly defined, of deep internal conflict. She can be very gay, or sad to the point of anguish, or stony with piety. She gazes at her lovers now with perplexity, now with wild fear, but nearly always her gaze is strange. The fascination is frustrating enough while the princess is in love with Kirsanov, but when her passion ceases her lover is plunged into utter torment. When she goes abroad he abandons his career to follow her, spends years in the pursuit. He is humiliated, indignant with himself, tried to break off but always fails. "Her image, that incomprehensible *well-nigh meaningless yet captivating image* had let roots far too deeply within his soul." The princess has a brief flare of revived emotion; it then expires forever, for her, but not for him.

The impression is strongly conveyed that it is mainly the "enigmatic look" which so intrigues the lover in this instance. The princess is a victim of internal stresses of no recognizable kind; her personality baffles, and we are left with the question whether mystery alone can account for a fixation of such power and endurance. It may be suggested that such a quality in itself might arouse a sustained interest, but not a passion, unless there was *some* kind or degree of esthetic appeal.* The point will be taken up later on.

* One of the classic literary treatments of amorous passion makes up a large part of the book *Of Human Bondage,* by Somerset Maugham (New York: Sun Dial Press, 1945), where the compulsive and irrational character of such a passion is emphasized. The striking feature in this instance, however, is the almost entirely negative image of the love-object. Apart from a brief reference to her profile, every feature is unattractive. She is very thin, narrow-hipped, flat-chested and anemic. Her skin has a faintly greenish tint, her mouth is thin, pale, and ugly. Her personality has no single redeeming trait; she is vulgar, ignorant, unfriendly, snobbish, mentally dull, without interest in world events, reads nothing but trash. She is emotionally cold, without kindness, mercy or charity. Maugham represents the attraction as a quite mysterious phenomenon, seeking, it would seem, to convey to the reader that an inexplicable force is at work by making the girl as repellent as possible. He apparently agrees with his hero: "He did not know what it was that passed from a man to a woman, from a woman to a man, and made one of them a slave; it was convenient to call it the sexual instinct, but if it was no more than that, he did not understand why it should

A final example may serve to bring the fetish concept into the sphere of normality. Although the theme of H. H. Richardson's novel *Maurice Guest* (1930) presents little of unusually dramatic character it is for that reason suitable at this point; it has also the merit of summarizing all of the essentials of pure amorous esthetics as we have outlined them.

Maurice is a student of music at Leipzig near the end of the nineteenth century. The story begins with his encounter with another student, Louise, at the home of his professor:

> And now came for him one of those moments in life which, unlooked-for, undivined, send before them no promise of being different, in any way, from the commonplace moments that make up the balance of our days. No gently graduated steps lead up to them: they are upon us with the violent abruptness of a streak of lightning. (p. 28)

For an instant the face fails to register, then his attention is fixed "with an intentness that . . . feverishly grew, until he could not tear his eyes away." The girl's features, we are told, are far from perfect, without charm of line or symmetry, but for him they are to the highest degree intriguing, exotic. Black, luxuriant hair is noted, but it is her eyes that affect him most. He knows nothing of the girl,

---

occasion so vehement an attraction to one person rather than another. It was irresistible: the mind could not battle with it; friendship, gratitude, interest, had not power beside it" (p. 429).

I suggest that while the power of the fixation has never been better described, it is not psychologically realistic and must be classed with the familiar tradition that such passions are mysteries beyond analysis. That a man may be enthralled by a woman *all* of whose traits are without appeal is to add paradox to mystification. The throes of the compulsion are vivid and memorable, but at core the account is false.

has never seen her before. Nothing is said about resemblances, or associations with known persons, or the expression of personal qualities. Yet, he knows that henceforth he will no longer be free, that a powerful new force has entered his life, that he cannot turn back; that, in short, he has "fallen in love."

The urge to see her again becomes obsessive and he haunts the neighborhood of the music school in the hope of a chance encounter. Long before he finally succeeds in meeting her, he suffers painful jealousy on glimpsing her with another man. Discovering where she lives, he studies her movements, the streets and place she frequents, learns to recognize her at great distances. He is aware that he is acting under compulsion.

Significant for our concept of amorous emotion is the fact that during the same period Maurice spends much time with another student, mainly because of her warm friendliness when he is lonely. This girl is kind, helpful, generous and perceptive. She is animated, intelligent, a stimulating companion. He finds her honesty "delightfully refreshing"; her voice and manner are pleasant. In brief, her personality is attractive to Maurice, yet she arouses no emotion whatever in him beyond friendliness. He never thinks of her when he is not with her. There is never a look, a smile, or a gesture that arouses amorous feeling. She provides an excellent example of an individual rich in social appeal but without esthetic attractiveness for him.

In sharp contrast, the distinctive allure of Louise colors everything she does, quite apart from her personal traits. "Hers was a nameless charm; it was present in each gesture of the slim hands, in each turn of the head, in every movement of the slender body." Her walk has the same quality: "there was something in the way her skirts clung, and moved with her, that was different from the motion of other women's."

Her eyes, "unfathomable," are the main source of the

effect she has upon Maurice: "not their size, or their dark brilliancy, but the manner of their setting: the spacious lid that fell from the high, wavy eyebrow, first sloping deeply inward, then curving out again over the eyeball; this, and the clean sweep of the broad, white lid, which, when lowered, gave the face an infantine look—a look of marble" (p. 550). Yet not the eyes alone, or the face; "it was also the line of the throat and chin, when she turned her head; it was the gesture with which she fingered the knot of hair on her neck; above all her hands, whose every movement was full of meaning . . ."

The power of the emotion aroused by these surface structures, which makes the main theme of the novel, is not supported by any deeper traits. There is an appealing candor about her, and she has some painfully won wisdom of living, but she is moody, inclined to be indolent, has few interests or emotional resources to sustain her, little to turn to during the intervals between love affairs. Maurice is repelled by what he learns of her amorous and sexual history. Sex itself, however, figures very little in the novel; the erotic note is infrequent and subdued; there is hardly any reference to Louise's body, apart from her grace of movement. Maurice marvels at the potency of her eyes, "more especially when, in the brain and soul that lay behind, no spiritual trait answered to the physical."

Maurice and Louise have little in common; so far as temperament and sympathies are concerned they do not really belong together. Yet so great is the power of her appeal for him that it far outlasts the tragic conflicts created by his jealousy that finally destroys the relationship. His need of her persists even when respect, trust and tenderness have been lost.

Maurice, however, is no fetishist in the abnormal sense, for the allure that Louise possesses for him often affects others as well. One of her former lovers describes well the subtlety of her magic, which she herself has learned to practice with skill.

Her instinct taught her what was required of her. She would fall into an attitude and remain motionless in it, as if she knew the eye must feast its fill. . . . If some of her ways of expressing herself in motion could be caught and fixed, a sculptor's fame would be made.—A painter's if he could reproduce the trick she has of smiling entirely with her eyes and eyebrows.—And then her hands. . . . She has only to raise them, to pass them over her forehead or to finger at her hair, and the world is hers.—Do you really think a man asks soul of a woman with such eyes and hands as those? (pp. 549–50)

The speaker is not only a perceptive lover; he is a philosopher of esthetics, too: "Spring, colour, light, music, perfume: they are all to be found in the curve of a perfect throat or arm" (p. 504).*

* The poets, as might be expected, have supplied their own expressions of the same thesis. Here the eighteenth-century poet Bürger testifies to his bafflement as well as his fascination, and illustrates Stekel's observation that one may be aware of the source but not *recognize* it as such.

You're not homely, that is true!
You've an eye that's clear and blue;
Cunning mouth and little nose
Have their merits, I suppose.
Charming is the word to fit it,—
Yes, you're charming; I admit it.

Charming here and charming there,
But no *empress* anywhere
No! I cannot quite allow
Beauty's crown would suit your brow.
Charming there and charming here
Do not make a queen, my dear.

The role of expression, of the eyes in particular but also of the features as a whole, is emphasized far more than any other specific trait in both fictional and factual accounts of amorous fixation. What is *expressed* may of course be any one or more of the socially desirable traits of personality; most commonly candor, humor, animation or amiability. Since traits of this kind and many others comparable in positive values *do not differentiate the sexes,* they can only reinforce but not create amorous emotion: one does not fall in love with such behavior, however attractive and highly valued. However closely the expression of such qualities may blend with those of the esthetic surfaces, only

---

For I know a hundred girls,
Brown as berries, fair as
     pearls,
Each of whom might claim the
     prize
Given to loveliest lips and
     eyes—
Yes, a hundred might go in,
Challenge you, sweet child,
     and win.

A hundred beauties, did I say?
Why, what a number! Yet
     there may
A hundred thousand girls
     combine
To drive thee from this heart
     of mine:
May try together, try alone,—
My empress they cannot de-
     throne.

Roguish lip and roguish eye,
Look at me and make reply.
Witch! I wish to understand
How I came into your hand.
Look at me and make reply:
Tell me, roguish lip and eye.

Up and down I search to see.
The meaning of this mystery.
Tied so tight by *nothing,* dear?
Ah! there must be magic here!
Up and down, sweet sorceress,
     tell!
Where's your wand, and
     what's your spell?

G. A. Bürger, "The Witch," trans. J. F. Clarke, in *An Editor's Treasury* (New York: Atheneum, 1968, p. 1775).

a response of some degree to the latter can arouse the romantic mood.

In Malamud's story we are told that there is something very strange about the eyes of Finkle's enchantress, recalling a part of the romantic tradition which sometimes hinted—or even made explicit—that only an indefinable quality of some kind could account for the vastly impressive power of the emotion—at least in some instances. Must there be something enigmatic, a touch of the indefinable, to awaken the emotion in its romantic, or irrational form, and might this be even the mark that defines it as "romantic"?

Doubtless there are many who would prefer to think of attraction itself as a unique phenomenon beyond analysis. It is more romantic to regard it as a product of forces that impel toward each other by deep affinities or that we are somehow predestined to meet and marry the right lover. It has even been a part of popular philosophy that sexual love is not "the real thing" if a person knows precisely why he feels as he does.

The belief in irrational attraction is well enough established to prompt a brief inquiry as to its origin. If emphasis on a high degree of individuality—or of minor fetishisms—in sex esthetics is warranted, one would expect the romantic tradition to include the tenet that choices will often appear strange. People who do *not* respond emotionally where others do are perhaps bound to find such attractions somewhat baffling and therefore unreasonable. It will be a different matter, of course, where several or many agree in their appreciation and thus establish an "acknowledged" beauty.

A prominent writer in this field of behavior believes that "most people are unaware of their fetishisms. This is what endows the sudden falling in love with a sense of mystery in the minds of lovers. They do now know that what at-

tracted and bound them to their love objective was a particular . . . bodily part, some characteristic gesture or
motion, and they rationalize this attraction by referring to
psychic qualities such as similar tastes, mutual understanding, harmonious convictions, etc." (Stekel, 1927, p. 39).
Add to this that a certain detachment is needed for this
kind of analysis, and that a person under the influence of
strong emotion is not likely to be in a frame of mind favorable to it.

It is undeniable that anything suggestive of mystery may
be intriguing and can stimulate the imagination in this
region of experience as it does in others. But mystery
alone does not cause amorous arousal; indeed, it has not
been demonstrated that mystery, in the sense of unexplored features or facets of personality, is a real essential
to sexual love. Certain persons of whom we lack full knowledge may well be potential sources of undefined and intriguing impressions, but *these do not become important to us,* in
a sexual relationship, *unless attraction has already been felt.*

CHAPTER 6

The Role of Esthetic
Attraction in Mate
Selection

Most of the considerable research into the reasons why
people marry has been done by sociologists, rather than by
psychologists; as a result, there has been little study of the
emotional factors involved in marital choice. Until very
recently sexual *love* would not have been taken seriously as
a topic for investigation. Indeed, psychologists "did not
themselves acknowledge the legitimacy of investigating
passionate love. They often ridiculed colleagues who began conducting experiments on this topic. To study love
was to be 'soft-headed,' 'unscientific,' or to possess a flair
for the trivial" (Walster, 1971, p. 86).

Many observations have been made concerning the
meager research on romantic love; it is paradoxical that
this scholarly taboo should exist in a society which accepts
romantic love as the normal and necessary preface to marriage—the most important of all human relationships.

> The mate selection process has been widely investi-
> gated, and a number of promising theories . . . have
> been developed. The focus of these . . . however, is
> not the romantic element per se except insofar as the
> latter is held to derive from the theoretical factors . . .

under consideration. . . . . We know next to nothing . . . about the frequency or intensity of love among the various population elements. We do not know whether there are significant age and sex differences or whether there is correlativity between love and such variables as personality type, I.Q., social class, marital status, and other components of behavior routinely studied by students of the family. (Kephart, 1967, p. 470)

There is most certainly a sociology of sexual love, and several books have been written on the many influences which have entered into its status or rating in any given culture as a part of human life. Granted that there is a "pure" sex-esthetic emotion, the way it is experienced will always be affected to some degree by the consensus of each age as to what it means and how important an experience it is. William James, in reviewing a book that regarded romantic love as a new development in human emotional history, pointed out the difference between emotion as an experience and as a *value* of the age and the society in which it occurs (James, 1887). An attraction in a cultural setting in which woman is valued much less than man will not register with the same impact as one in which, with the same esthetic response, woman is respected and the emotion idealized.

James's conclusion was that an emotion as powerful as the romantic fixation could hardly be a recent addition to the human repertoire. In all ages, he suggested, feminine beauty has created amorous longings among men, but the total effect differs, for example, in a society in which emotional calm and stoic detachment are ideals, and in a romantic one such as ours. A history of the amorous experience itself, Aldous Huxley once suggested, might be written in terms of vogues, styles, or fashions; the basic experience does not change, but each age tends to perceive, value and express it differently (Huxley, 1930, pp. 144–45). Those inclined to see social influences as always strongly predominant in human behavior might even interpret ancient Greek homoeroticism as proving that custom is potent enough to alter the basic direction of romantic attraction.

In America the more sober tradition of mate selection was not markedly romantic during the nineteenth century. A British observer is quoted: "Love, among the American people, appears to be regarded rather as an affair of the judgment, than of the heart; its expression seems to spring from a sense of duty, rather than from a sentiment of feeling" (Murstein, 1971, p. 100). Marriage manuals of the period emphasized religion, health, morality, character, and absence of vices as the primary considerations for marital choice. Eventually the principle of similarity moved into the foreground as the basis of compatibility. It was soon supplemented by that of "complementarity," meaning that deficits or excesses should be compensated by opposite characteristics in the mate. A timid husband, for example, should have a courageous wife; extravagance in one should be balanced by caution in the other. One should seek in a mate, therefore, someone similar in age, race, religion, education, and social background, but different in character in a way that would counterbalance one's deviations from desirable standards.

Some present-day views of mate selection may be briefly outlined to show the place of esthetic-romantic attraction within the larger setting of factors that determine marital choice.

There is much evidence that people who marry resemble each other in a number of ways to a greater degree than would be accounted for by chance (Burgess and Wallin, 1943, 1944; Burgess and Locke, 1960). The likenesses, or *tendencies* toward likeness, include physical attractive-

ness, stature, eye and hair color, intelligence and education, "income brackets," religion, and certain traits of
personality. To a considerable degree, thus, the popular
notion that "similars attract" has been confirmed.

The word "tendencies" is emphasized to indicate that
such findings mean only that similarities are more often
found than differences among those who mate. Unlike
traits may not only be present, but some of them may add
to attraction. Unlikeness might even be more common
among people who attract but do not marry. The main
finding is that when they do marry, resemblances of various kind outnumber the differences.

Does this mean that people who attract each other
enough to marry do so *because* of the similarities, or is
there another way of accounting for the findings?

Before there can be attraction there must be encounter,
and studies of the "geography" of marriage have shown
that people who live near each other are more likely to
meet; here again a tendency that allows for many exceptions (Brossard, 1940; Davis and Reeves, 1939). On balance the number of matings decreases as the distance
between homes increases. Other things being equal, one is
more likely to become acquainted with someone in the
same block than with a person who lives a mile away, since
one is more likely to attend the same church or neighborhood meeting places.

Another finding is that people who live near each other
tend toward likeness in race, nationality, religion, income,
and educational level (Davis and Reeves, 1939; Murdoch,
1949; Nimkoff, 1947). People of eastern European background, for example, settled and employed in an industri-
al area, will be more like each other than like people in a
suburb inhabited mainly by workers in business offices.
Combining the two findings, there will obviously be a

greater likelihood that people similar in race, nationality, religion, and income level will get acquainted than will those who differ in these ways. Marriages between people of areas differing greatly in such characteristics are rare. Many of the similarities between mates are thus no more than the result of the relationship between "like people in like places." If Scandinavians tend to settle near each other it will not mean sexual choice alone when the members of a mating pair are both blue-eyed blondes. For the same reason, a boy and girl who meet at college or at a private golf club will contribute to the trend that marriage partners are similar in education and income.

The many exceptions to these trends are significant for the problem of sexual choice. When people attract each other strongly *despite* many differences, sexual choice stands out clearly as a psychological phenomenon. It is equally clear, though less striking of course, when people who are alike in many ways fail to attract each other. Certainly the many attractions which *deviate* from the norms suggest some factor of considerable potency, and this in turn may be related to the question of what determines choice when all the similarity factors are present and seem to be equally favorable. Choices which may be immediate and strongly felt do occur even in groups in which the similarity factors are numerous and prominent.

Inquiries into the expressed preferences of young people regarding the place of esthetic attractiveness in mate selection have often found attraction secondary to traits of personality and social assets, emotional responsiveness, "family-mindedness," and home-making interests. It is doubtful, however, that such findings fully reveal the role of physical attractiveness, as several students have acknowledged. The young have absorbed from our culture not only the romantic image of marriage but also a compensating bias toward more practical considerations favorable to congenial companionship, security, and stability. Those being interviewed easily recognize the "right answers" to questionnaires, knowing that an overemphasis on surface attraction is considered naive and immature, a sign of infatuation, not love. To be influenced more by charm than by solid marital assets is to place youthful and short-term considerations before more lasting and "wiser" ones.

One may know how a wise choice is made, however, and fully intend to make it, but discover oneself acting on quite different grounds. Nonsexual factors may be in the foreground of the findings on mating preferences, yet many of the traits with high ratings in such surveys can not be discerned until young people have been together for some time. What brings them together at the outset must be some degree of initial attraction in which surface traits figure most prominently. Whether attraction *continues* will then be determined to an important degree by nonsexual personality factors.

In emphasizing sexual esthetics, we do not assert that it is central to every attraction. That it may often be low in potency is suggested by the apparently slow growth of amorous emotion in many courtships, some surveys having shown that the majority of mates have known each other a year or more before the final commitment is made. Sudden and rapidly developing fixations in which surface allure predominates over all else are certainly not common. Attachments are unquestionably formed in the relative absence of strong esthetic appeals, and these may be truly *love* relationships. They do not, however, represent amorous emotion as defined in this book. They include little of the romantic experience.

A number of theories have been proposed and examined in the literature on marital choice.* It has been suggested, for example, that selection will be importantly determined not only by romantic attraction but by the attracted person's estimate of his own assets compared with those of the object of his interest. He will be influenced by the likelihood of his acceptance if he makes an approach. The outcome might thus show a considerable difference between the person *desired* and the person *chosen,* as when the attracted person rates himself low in assets, or when the competition is intense. Realistic and idealistic choices, in other words, may markedly differ. An often-quoted statement in this context has been made:

> A proposal of marriage in our society tends to be a way in which a man sums up his social attributes and suggests to a woman that hers are not so much better as to preclude a merger or partnership in these matters. (Goffman, 1952, p. 451)

* Among the more prominent theories of mate selection, apart from the Freudian, is that of "complementary needs," meaning that choice is importantly influenced when a person finds satisfaction of his unfulfilled emotional needs in the personality of another (Winch, 1958, 1967). The satisfactions may be the same for both, or they may differ, but the attractive traits or qualities provide what each feels to be lacking.

Another theory is based on the correspondence between an image of the ideal mate and the characteristics of the person encountered, with the degree of attraction depending on how closely the ideal is approached. An often-cited research discovered that over three-quarters of a group of college men did have such an ideal, and that about half acknowledged making the comparison in selecting a mate (Strauss, 1946).

Both formulations have been regarded as plausible, and both, like most others, have met with critical reactions and some negative findings, when tested.

The few experiments directly designed to test the role of the "esthetic surface" have brought out its importance. One of these, for example, on the basis of a relatively brief exposure in a controlled dating situation, established that "Sheer physical attraction appears to be the overriding determinant of liking," such attraction not being correlated with intelligence, personality traits, or the attracted person's estimate of his own desirability (Walster et al., 1966). The findings of studies made under the necessarily brief periods of such controlled conditions might admittedly be different with longer acquaintance, and the effects of non-physical traits would be expected to be greater.*

Further illustrations of the psychology of the amorous experience range from the theory that the important factors are unconscious and therefore not open to the usual scientific methods, or are mainly a matter of pure chance —simply "who *happens* to meet whom"—all the way to the view that choice represents the more or less calculated outcome of a balancing of positive and negative elements, a weighing of assets versus liabilities, compatibilities versus incompatibilities, etc.† Many of the suggestions are plausi-

* There have been many studies of the general phenomenon of interpersonal attraction, but the majority have focused on social attraction, or "liking," between individuals of the same sex, especially as seen in young people in the late teens and early twenties. Physical attractiveness has been found to be a factor of considerable importance in such relationships.

† The interpretation of amorous fixation offered in this book contrasts sharply with what may be termed the sociological view, an extreme form of which has been stated by I. L. Reiss. "The oft-asked question 'Why did this particular person fall in love with this other particular person?' can be answered by sociologists in terms of our approach. From our point of view, the love object could have been a number of people with similar socio-

ble and usually have *some* evidence to support them. One theory holds that people who mate tend to find emotional satisfaction of some one or more of their personal needs. Thus an insecure man needs a confident woman; or an emotionally dependent woman needs a "masterful" man. Such situations would of course exhibit many grades, and in practice the principle would mean simply that while nearly everyone seeks a mate who is physically attractive, intelligent, and stable, people will desire these traits to the degree to which they lack them themselves, or at least feel that they do. Among other possibilities the compatibility of *values* has been explored, meaning the relative importance, for each member of a pair, of major interests and life goals.

Some of the psychological factors underlying the findings have also been of interest; for example, *why* similarities should attract. Self-esteem, among other factors, has been found important, since it raises one's morale to find that an admired and respected person has values and attitudes in agreement with one's own. Self-esteem may also at outset have a part in the decision whether to approach an

---

cultural characteristics. *Chance* factors led to it being this particular person" (Reiss, 1960, p. 139).

This means that regardless of individuality, two people will fall in love if certain culturally determined personality traits happen to correspond, these being most importantly the ability to fulfill each other's needs, the inclination to reveal themselves to each other, rapport and so on. Reiss concedes that these elements are common to any close relationship, as between friends, or between parent and child, but that romantic love has a "specific meaning and content" that distinguishes it from all others. This approach fails to tell what this meaning and content are. There is certainly a sociology of love, but our thesis must be that a "pure" sociological bias will miss the essential factor in amorous emotion.

attractive person, since the possibility of rejection may have to be considered. People low in self-esteem "are less selective and aim lower in their interpersonal choices than do high self-esteem individuals" (Murstein, 1971, p. 128). I have seen, in many years of marriage analysis, tragic instances in which a person with conspicuous assets has, because of incompatibly low self-esteem, accepted a marital partner far inferior in favorable traits.

A variety of *compensating* factors are often at work in mate selection. An unattractive man may be acceptable to an attractive woman because of his favorable traits of personality, or because of the financial security he offers; differences in values may also be sacrificed for economic reasons. An educated man may accept a woman who cannot give him intellectual companionship but whom he finds very attractive physically. It has been found that a husband's superiority to his wife in social status is related to her physical assets; he is willing to concede the one in order to gain the other. On the whole, research in this field has resulted in some rather complex relationships among the variables, not all of which are fully understood.*

* The literature on mate selection strongly suggests an overall complex of many factors as basis of choice, though there may be few, of course, in any one instance. One study found degrees of support for a variety of hypotheses; among others, that premarital couples will tend to be similar in physical attractiveness and in attitudes and values; that there will tend to be agreement between the chosen person and the image of the ideal mate; that similarity in levels of self-acceptance will correlate with progress in courtship, this being also true of the level of neuroticism (Murstein, 1971, pp. 137–47). The investigator in this instance suggests, as a line of further research, that explorations be made of the different *kinds* of individuals who make their choices on the primary basis of similarity of values, compatibility of roles in marriage, emphasis on the externals of attraction, etc.

As an example of an approach to the problem of mate selection one of the earlier theories—still widely current—may be briefly outlined. Among the more popular doctrines of the origins of the love-choice has been that of the Freudian school, based on the familiar Oedipus complex. In this view the erotic life begins in infancy and is first awakened by the mother, whose caresses and other contacts in caring for the child are sexually stimulating. In this way it comes about, according to Freudian theory, that the infant boy's earliest love-object is his own mother. For the girl it is the father, though this "choice" arises in a different way. It is in the family, in the prolonged and close contact between child and parent, that the root of later preferences is planted. The boy will be predisposed toward persons like his mother, the girl toward someone like her father. Stressed in this account is the great importance of *primacy,* or "firstness," meaning that the experiences of early life are much more likely to determine adult behavior than are later ones.

Any preferences the parent of opposite sex expresses toward the child—the father finding more pleasure in the girl, the mother in the boy—are seen as supporting the original fixation. Should an adolescent boy's first amorous experience involve an older woman, it would appear to illustrate the effect of the mother-image. As the child matures he is from time to time attracted to members of the opposite sex outside the family and more nearly his own age. With these experiences the process of emotional weaning from the parental first love gets under way. When and if it is completed, later sexual preferences may be free of the parental influence, but in many instances the latter may be strong enough, according to the doctrine, to affect markedly the direction of amorous interest and marital choice.

If this were true we should expect some degree of resemblance, physical or mental, between the attractive person and the opposite-sex parent. The influence might be active without awareness on the part of the affected person, since people are often unable to say with any assurance why they are attracted to a particular person. The younger the child, however, the more his love interest would tend toward a parent or an older adult. A study of the amorous behavior of school children which included a few of preschool age was cited earlier. It showed that very young children may exhibit attractions which may be quite strong, the objects being of opposite sex, of comparable age, and *outside* the family—a line of evidence which clearly fails to support the theory.

Direct comparisons between mates and opposite-sex parents have also failed to support it. The results of several investigations have revealed that mates of attractive persons are more often unlike parents than like them. Marked degrees of resemblance were found in only a small minority of instances (Burgess and Cottrell, 1939; Davis and Reeves, 1939; Hamilton, 1929; Kirkpatrick, 1937; Terman, 1938).

Such findings cannot be conclusive for a theory which assumes influences of this kind to be active mainly at an unconscious level. It is not agreed by all investigators that such influences must necessarily be unconscious, but it is often hard for adults to make comparisons between their mates and their parents as they remember them to have been in childhood. The doctrine does not, however, state that parent-resemblance is the only factor in mate selection, since one may outgrow this influence and choice may then be made on different grounds.

A more basic weakness in the parent-image theory has been pointed out. To compare a male infant's feelings for his mother with an adult male's attraction to a mature woman raises an obvious question: are these the same *kind* of feelings? If not, the maternal attachment of the infant would not be expected to influence the mating choice of the adult. For Freudians the answer is clear: the infant desires his mother sexually; therefore his adult sex desire can be directly influenced by the mother-image. That the adult may be in love as well as sexually aroused does not affect the issue, since for Freudians the amorous emotion is largely a by-product of inhibition.

The question then becomes whether the infant's emotional fixation on his mother is truly erotic. That he literally desires his mother sexually has emphatically not been generally accepted by psychologists outside of the Freudian school. A factor in this peculiar doctrine was Freud's idea that *all* affectional expression is basically sexual, with sublimation as the transformer for the different experiences. Freud's thesis was supported by the similarity of sexual and affectional *behavior:* since both tend toward physical contact—caresses, kissing—the erroneous deduction was made: like behavior, like motive.*

Until it can be shown to be otherwise, it can be assumed

*A medical roundtable discussion of falling in love (*Medical Aspects of Human Sexuality 3* [New York: Clinical Communications, September 1969] illustrates the still common failure to distinguish between amorous emotion and the bond between parent and child, it being implied that the latter is basic to the possibility of future amorous attraction. "Unless one has been loved as a child, one can neither seek love nor give it effectively as an adult. The roots of future love relationships lie in the earliest mother-child unity . . ." Features of amorous behavior without parallel in the parent-child relationship are discussed with no apparent awareness that the two experiences do not correlate.

Our treatment does not deny that the ability to form adult love bonds may be vitally influenced by the quality of those within the family. It proposes only that the amorous emotion is itself in an altogether different mode, and one requiring a different vocabulary.

that the child's response to his mother's affection and the adult's amorous response to his sweetheart or mate are not the same experience, just as it is assumed that the mother's affection for her child and her amorous response to her husband are two different motives *because they are of different quality as feelings.* Both may be classed as "love," but in this sphere of the emotional life feelings may differ widely, yet bear the same label.

A different view of the parent-image theory is possible if we consider the child's dependent attitude toward its parents. Maternal affection, in making the child feel safely protected, will cause his security needs to be associated with them, and with the love they express. Later, as an adult, if security needs are still active, we may expect him to seek a person resembling the parent as a likely source of the same kind of satisfaction he received in infancy.

This would be a parent-determined love choice, but it would clearly not be the kind that has been central in our discussion. It is not unusual for an emotionally dependent person to be in need of a parent substitute in his choice of mate, and often to continue to express this need in marriage. What is stressed here is that the amorous kind of love choice is not to be understood in terms of the parent image when its emotional quality is entirely different.

The many findings among factors making for compatibility in marriage—similarities of values, goals and interests; correspondence in concepts of roles; agreement and disagreement with the "ideal image"; various compensatory elements—all rest upon the essential premise that the pairs have been together long enough to discover these qualities and relationships. A basic question clearly remains: what brings them together and keeps them together long enough to make possible this kind of mutual knowledge? That there must be at least surface attraction is usually taken for granted in such studies but is rarely acknowledged as itself a possible primary factor in marital choice.*

A recent investigator concedes that in the first phase of attraction "visual and auditory" factors—appearance and voice—are vital. He concedes also that this phase is of "crucial importance," since if it fails, the further contacts which would reveal other facets of personality will not be sought. "While the 'prospect' . . . might potentially be a highly desirable person with compatible values, the individual—foregoing opportunities for further contact—never finds this out. In consequence, it would appear that physically unattractive individuals are at a considerable handicap" (Murstein, 1971, p. 112).†

In centering attention on the response to esthetic individuality as primary in attraction and in marital choice

* A few of the earlier workers in the field of marriage have seen nonsexual factors as reinforcing or reducing the attraction first determined by physical characteristics. There is evidence which "would seem to show that a person's first concern in mate selection is to seek out those persons who meet his general physical standard. Once this has been accomplished his selection of a mate is made from this group on the basis of the specific personality characteristics which he desires in a mate. Thus physical characteristics may be the initial selective factors within which personality discrimination takes place" (Lantz and Snyder, 1962, p. 147).

† Professor Murstein writes: "If marital choice depended only on . . . attractiveness . . . we would have a largely unmarried population, since everyone would be drawn toward the relatively few highly attractive persons" (p. 112). The research findings make it clear that there are other factors of importance, but his statement overlooks the fundamental fact of individuality in sex-esthetic choice. Otherwise it would be assumed that the great majority must accept esthetically unattractive mates, meaning, in our view, marriages without amorous emotion ("falling in love").

there is no intention here to oversimplify the highly complex psychology of sexual selection. A variety of motivating factors must be considered in any inclusive study; circumstances as well as interpersonal interests have a role. The "marriage of convenience" will of course always be with us. Sheer physical sexuality is surely often foremost, while large allowance must be made for the social needs and compatibilities with which many courtships begin, and which may be said to define the majority of successful marriages after the inherently transient romantic phase subsides. Romantic love, as one student says, "for all its height, has little depth or breadth."

It remains true, however, and very importantly true, that attraction, whatever its course, begins with surface esthetics, which provide the necessary condition for much of the interactions that follow. There has rarely been any question as to what sustains the marital bond after years of cohabitation. The basic question about "this thing called love" has centered on the roots of choice in attraction. In its "irrationality," choice has always been the fundamental mystery of the relationship between man and woman.

CHAPTER 7

Sexual Love: Instinct or Cultural Learning?

Much of the literature of sex psychology states or implies that the attraction of the sexes is entirely a matter of learning. It is conceded, of course, that in the early months of life the male infant is erotically sensitive; there may be erections, with reflex movements of the pelvic musculature, and continued stimulation may elicit orgasm. At puberty organic changes occur in response to the chemistry of the growth processes.

According to much current doctrine all or nearly all sexual behavior beyond these elements is a product of experience. The small boy at first makes little distinction between the sexes. Girls are not yet attractive objects. Gradually his perception of them changes as he learns in a variety of ways that they are sources of a unique pleasure. Eventually he experiences this pleasure in erotic contact and henceforth becomes sexually excitable by those features of the female body in which it differs from the male. All of the genital and emotional effects of perception of and contact with the opposite sex are assumed to be learned, either directly or through social conditioning.

The truth of these statements regarding the learning of sexual responses has never been demonstrated. There has been little movement in this region of sexual theory, and many psychologists would today agree with what a specialist on emotion wrote 40 years ago: "The halo of perfection and charm which would seem to surround the object of sex attraction is . . . entirely a matter of learning" (Lund, 1930, p. 177). This means, we must suppose, that the sexes are lacking in interest to each other until, through instruction or experience, they come to be perceived as sources of pleasure. The same writer states, however, that there is an esthetic response between males and females and that we must distinguish between "attraction stimuli" and "sex stimuli." There is an interest which is sexual in that it is aroused by the opposite sex, but different in that it does not stimulate the genitals; it is "without direct sex value" (p. 232).

Here is an admission that there are two different kinds of sexual attraction, one esthetic and the other not, yet the assertion that all attraction comes from erotic pleasure gives no basis for such a dichotomy. Other examples could be cited of the difficulties of building a consistent sex psychology without fully facing the fact that attraction is of two different modes.

Direct evidence that the esthetic attraction of the sexes is unlearned lies in what has for ages been obvious to everyone—that a boy need not be taught what a pretty girl looks like, nor that some girls are, to him, prettier than others, any more than he needs to be taught that flowers, sunsets, and landscapes may be beautiful, or that certain patterns of line and color are pleasing to the eye. Granted that social standards may markedly affect individual judgments of beauty; but not all esthetic appreciation in the sexual sphere is itself of cultural origin.

Indirect evidence of the unlearned character of normal attraction includes the almost universal difference between the sexes in the esthetic response: that beauty is typically a feminine attribute, that it is woman who displays it and man who seeks it. If, as will later be suggested, the homosexual inclination—which so often appears to develop spontaneously and persistently manifests itself against the current of social influence—is in large part unlearned, it may be inferred that normal attractions of the same quality—response to personal esthetics—are also unlearned, at least pending adequate evidence to the contrary.

The view that the appreciation of sexual beauty is rooted in an inborn specialization of human esthetic sensibility would appear to be at once challenged by the difference among various human societies in standards of attractiveness, which by some have been taken to mean that esthetic preferences are entirely a matter of social custom. Such variations are what would be expected, however, if we assume that while culture may modify preferences, it does not *create* esthetic sensibility in the sexual realm, any more than it creates the response to musical tones.* A youth's preferences, as he matures, may change in the direction of the values of his social environment, but he does not have to wait, so to speak, until his culture tells him that one person is more attractive than another before he finds his interest aroused by *certain individuals.* Occasionally, in fact, he may respond with remarkable intensity in the apparent

---

* Havelock Ellis, after a thorough survey, concluded that there are common factors underlying the variations in standards of sexual beauty, noting that Europeans often find the women of primitive societies attractive while the males of such peoples have expressed admiration for women of European cultures. "When we survey broadly the ideals of feminine beauty set down by peoples of many lands, it is interesting to note that they all contain many features which appeal to the aesthetic taste of the modern European, and many of them . . . contain no features which obviously clash with his canons of taste" (Ellis, 1936, I, 3:151).

absence of any such influence or instruction. The literature of biography and autobiography is rich in examples of this kind. Often they occur at an early age, and far more often suggest spontaneous appreciation than mere recognition of socially approved types. Despite whatever tendency there may be toward consensus within a given society, there will also be a broad range of individuality of the kind which may be illustrated in the judgment: I recognize that "A" is more beautiful than "B" by current standards, but I prefer "B" nevertheless.

The romantic experience, someone has said, is the poetry of the unpoetic—that is, those without the capacity for the appreciation of other arts respond esthetically to sexual beauty. Surveys of the frequency of amorous experience among college students have shown that the emotion is by no means a rarity at this level of our society. It is highly unlikely that the topic itself, as represented in countless novels, popular fiction, and motion pictures, could arouse as nearly universal a response as it does were it other than a fairly common event. If interest in any theme or narrative means that we can share the related emotions to some degree, it follows that most people have some capacity for amorous emotion.

Since, however, individuals differ in every human capacity, it is quite safe to say that the esthetic-amorous response must range from a classic immediate, dramatic, and powerful fixation, to a weak admiration adding little to basic genital-sexual interest. In some the perception of sexual beauty will arouse little more than the impulse toward sexual contact. For these people, much of this book would have small meaning and might seem to be concerned largely with incidental overtones of sensual activity and feelings.

That the growth of the amorous emotion is the cumulative effect of repeated esthetic responses to a *selected* individual is our main thesis concerning sexual love. Little is known as to how this comes about as a process within the organism. A student of emotional psychology has suggested that hatred, for example, is more enduring than anger, and "has the tendency to become almost a chronic emotional state, which is sustained by special thoughts." This is an excellent description of amorous emotion. Its growth will depend on the number of attractive traits and on the strength of the responses to them; it will be aided by attractive nonsexual traits; it will be slowed or checked by esthetically or socially unattractive ones.

The role of nonsexual attraction may in a given case be primary. Studies of preferences in mate selection have shown that many young people are aware that making a "wise" choice (as versus a merely romantic one) is vital for marriage as a companionship. This is the *rational* way, and attention to its guidelines is highly regarded for the prospects of a stable marriage. It is clearly not *amorous* choice as treated in this book. It is not the romantic experience.

The Sexual Complex

It has been stressed that the theory of sexual love as no more than a derived and altered form of the sexual impulse is greatly oversimplified. The facts are that there are two different kinds of sexual perception within the normal range, and two corresponding emotional states. Any tendency to reject this basic dualism on the grounds that it "complicates" sexual psychology must clearly bypass many other findings. Human sexual behavior is a complex of variables. Sexual anatomy, the direction of attraction, and sexual identity, for example, are to various degrees independent. Having the body of a male need not mean feeling like one, and feeling male does not always imply preference for the opposite sex. Most males who identify as males are attracted to women, but some are attracted to other males, and some who feel male are attracted to both sexes. There have been many who strongly desired a complete change of sex. A male may delight in his sex organs or find them repellent. Similarly, some females are content with their identities but are attracted to other females, and some feel like males and are attracted to women as men are.

Underlying the many influences of the social environment, all of which tend to mold behavior in the direction of what is considered normal, there appear to be at the base of sexuality certain root factors. Each is variable in strength, and each represents *potential* for development. Every male, for example, is expected to learn the masculine role. If his learning potential is adequate he will find it easy and congenial, and with superior potential he will learn it as a talented person learns an art. If potential is weak the learning will be slow and uncongenial, "against the grain," like an artistically inclined boy forced to learn law or a commercial vocation (e.g., Keats in medical school). Individual differences are found in every measurable learning capacity.

Thus variation in sexual identity, in attraction, and in interest show that sexual makeup is far from a unified construction. It is definitely not all of a piece, but rather a loosely knit complex.*

* Human physical sexuality is also an organization of separable parts: the external and internal genital structures, the glands, the hormones, and the genes, or units which transmit inheritance. Any one of these may be out of alignment with the rest. A child may be born female in all physical structures but one: the external genitals may be so masculinized that the infant is identified as male. The internal sex organs may be male, the external female (Money, 1961, p. 483).

The independence of amorous and genital-sexual attraction is but one of many examples. Biologically considered, esthetic allure is a means of bringing the sexes together for physical contact. It is a preliminary, without meaning apart from the goal of reproduction. As an *experience,* however, it may be an end in itself, and it may develop long before reproductive maturity.

Male and Female Responses

Given the male preoccupation with beauty, and the fact that beauty is primarily a feminine attribute, we would expect to find a difference in the two sexes' experience of sexual love. The usual statement is that the masculine role is to be attracted to one perceived as beautiful and to desire possession. Marriage, from the male viewpoint, reflects the urge to make such possession permanent. Woman's role, on the other hand, includes the enjoyment of *being* attractive and desired, the gratification of being highly valued and of belonging to her admirer. Closely related is the "need to be needed," it being part of woman's maternal nature to respond to her mate as she does to her family.

According to this view, then, the experience of a woman in love is narcissistic in that she is regarded as a precious and charming object, and takes pleasure in giving herself to one she accepts, and who strongly desires to possess her entire self. For man the core of the *romantic* state is the

---

Functions may also illustrate partial independence. There may be climax without ejaculation, or both without orgasmic sensation; the latter may occur in the absence of erection. Sexual desire may long outlive the physical reactions which make satisfaction possible. Many disharmonies of growth have been noted, different parts of the sexual system reaching maturity at different times.

lure of the beautiful and the hope of possession. But this contrast between the two sexes' experience is too sharp. The male ego can hardly fail to be gratified when accepted by a highly valued person, and it is doubtful that a woman is ever entirely unresponsive to the esthetic appeal of the male; rarely is an unattractive man the hero of a romance, and a handsome man may be assumed to have similar meaning to a woman as does a beautiful woman to a man. To the degree that these elements enter into attraction, it may be said that both sexes share in the romantic experience.

At this point, however, it is the difference that must be regarded as one of the essentials of sexual love, since a large enough difference in degree, in an emotional experience, may approach a difference in *kind.* It is, moreover, a difference that might have been anticipated in view of numerous other basic differences between the sexes in the large field of sexual behavior. Some of these have long been familiar and are well in line with the general principle that the role of the male is more active, that of the female more passive.

The material collected by the Kinsey researchers made clear that men and women differ greatly in responsiveness to sexual stimulation (Kinsey et al., 1953). Males react much more, for example, to photos and paintings of the nude female than do females to those of the nude male. More than half of 617 women reported that they had never been erotically aroused at sight of the male genitals, while few of the men in the sample had failed to be excited in this way (p. 655). Similar differences were found in the effect of observing sexual activity in others, or in response to public performances specialized for erotic stimulation. Males also respond more than females to fantasies of sexual experience, and far more males than females reported erotic dreams, and such dreams much more often led to climax.

Can differences in the upbringing and education of the sexes account for these data? Do they correspond to social influences that place greater emphasis on sexual and emotional control in the case of women? The answer may have a bearing on the differences in the character of the experience in sexual love.

A central finding of the Kinsey investigation (1953) with regard to sex differences is the far greater tendency of the male to respond to stimulation assumed to have been *associated* through experience with sexual pleasures. Of 33 bodies of data examined, 29 showed that "the male is conditioned by sexual experience more frequently than the female"; in 12 categories this difference was very large. (pp. 651–89). There is, in other words, a marked difference in the amount of "sexual learning" that has occurred, raising the issue whether these differences can be entirely explained by differences in opportunity to learn.

It is a striking fact that the same kinds of sex differences are observable in the lower animals. "The males of practically all infrahuman species may become aroused when they observe other animals in sexual activity" (p. 661). The females of these species, like the human female, are less responsive to such stimulation. It is reported of a number of subhuman species that the female animal shows less interest than the male in the genitalia of the opposite sex. A number of observers have been impressed by the greater excitability of the male animal by stimuli associated with sex. "Comparable conditioning," according to Ford and Beach (1951), "has never been observed in lower mammalian females" (p. 241). They note also the greater tendency of males, in all human societies for which data is available, to stimulate their own sex organs. They regard it as of "particular significance" that this is also true of many lower species. The greater occurrence of homosexual behavior in males as compared with females is found to be true for all other primate species. The same observers state: "We are strongly impressed with the evidence for sexual conditioning in the male and the relative absence of such processes in the female" (p. 241). Such similarities between man and the lower animals are numerous enough, they think, to indicate a basic pattern of sexual behavior to some degree common to both.

The use of parallels between human and animal behavior for their bearing on of what is learned or unlearned is generally regarded as a questionable practice. In this instance, however, the specific character of some of the numerous resemblances is highly suggestive. Another instance of this kind is the greater absorption of the human male in sexual activity. Once the erotic state is aroused it tends strongly to continue, but the female is much more easily distracted. "From the most ancient to the most modern erotic art, the female has been portrayed . . . as reading a book, eating, or engaged in other activities while she is in coitus; but no artist seems to have portrayed males engaged in such extraneous activities while in coitus." (Kinsey, 1953, p. 669). Similar behavior has been observed among subhuman species. "Cheese crumbs spread in front of a copulating pair of rats may distract the female, but not the male. A mouse running in front of a copulating pair of cats may distract the female, but not the male. When cattle are interrupted during coitus, it is the cow that is more likely to be disturbed while the bull may try to continue with coitus" (p. 669).

A frequent abnormality among males is public exposure of the genitals as a means of achieving erotic excitement. The writer has seen scores of these cases during 13 years

in a psychiatric clinic, but has never encountered this behavior in a female, nor reports of it in the literature on
sexual deviations. It is rare to find reports of erotic fetishism in women, and there is fair agreement that it is almost
exclusively male behavior. Sexual voyeurism is another example of typically male behavior, a finding well fitted to
other data when seen as an exaggerated development of
the normal response to visual stimulation. The transvestite
is almost always male (Benjamin, 1966, p. 31). Men much
more often desire a change of sex, despite the fact that
more women than men would prefer to have been born of
the opposite sex, presumably owing to the greater opportunities and freedom.

It is difficult to account for all of the findings on sex
differences in terms of the learning process. They might
be taken to show the male to have a remarkably greater
capacity for learning in the sex area, but this would be
close to assuming his sexual organization itself to be different. The alternative is to regard the differences as related
to our unquestionable hereditary relationship with the
lower animals. The correspondence of sex differences between animal and human behavior do not, of course,
prove a biological basis for the latter, but enough of them,
specific and all pointed in the same direction, must be
conceded as having weight. Consistent differences with regard to fetishism, voyeurism, transvestism, and transsex-
uality are similarly suggestive, or will be until adequate
evidence that learning experiences can account for them is
available. The assignment of all sex differences to cultural
factors leads, as usual, to the question of how these factors
originated if not in basic individual differences.

We conclude that until such sexual phenomena can be
shown to be learned, it is permissible to class them as in
part, at least, rooted in biology, and since the character of

the difference in esthetic-amorous behavior fits well into the overall patterns of unlikeness between man and woman, it can be similarly interpreted.

Attraction to the Same Sex

The phenomenon of attraction to the same sex is briefly included in this study for two reasons. It is, for a great many homosexuals, a *romantic* experience, involving the esthetic-amorous emotion as earlier defined. It also provides evidence bearing on the sources of normal attraction, the issue, for example, of whether one *learns* to find the opposite sex of interest—as some psychologists have proposed—or whether one is predisposed "by nature" to respond to it with pleasurable feelings.

Two features of homosexual behavior are important in the present context and may be briefly illustrated.

A youth of 23, who regards himself as a homosexual, stated:

> I guess I'm not very strongly sexed physically, but I'm very susceptible emotionally when I meet an attractive man. I'm very romantic. I fall hard, but all I really want is caressing and kissing and *possession.* When I'm in love I worry about losing my man and I'm inclined to be jealous.
>
> As far as sex is concerned it's the closeness that means most to me and giving pleasure to the other person. I could get along well enough with just the closeness, even without sex. My ideal is to find a lasting relationship. I mean someone to live with me. I'm tired of playing the field. I want to settle down with my loved one and be able to turn my mind to other things, like art and literature.
>
> My work involves being with girls and I like some of them very much but only as friends. I've never felt toward any of them the way I do about men.

Another young man consulted a psychologist about what he considered a strange and rather troubling emotional experience. He had seen a motion picture whose cast included the usual romantic pair; a beautiful star and her handsome leading man. He had found it stimulating but was startled to discover that he had reacted more strongly to the male than to the star. "It wasn't so much sexual as emotional," he explained; "I mean that this fellow had so much charm about him that I found I was looking at him more than at the woman. For several days afterward I had him on my mind." Despite his many attractions to girls and his quite normal sexual and emotional response to them he questioned whether he might not be a "latent homosexual."

A married man of 36, much in love with his wife and with considerable premarital sex experience with women, has been on several occasions strongly attracted to teenage boys. These have included physical relationships where possible. He is intelligent, aware of the risk entailed and distressed about the effect of the seductions upon the boys. He was finally detected, arrested, placed on probation, and advised to seek professional help.

These examples from the writer's file of cases observed in a clinical setting are intended at this point only to show that attraction to the same sex may be experienced by persons quite normally disposed toward the opposite sex; also that esthetic and amorous interest may be prominent in such attractions as well as the more common sensual or erotic variety.

We need to distinguish at the outset between homosexual behavior and attraction. Adolescent boys engaged in mutual masturbation, for example, are behaving sexually with a person of the same sex, but this behavior may be quite without bearing upon their basic sexuality. They may be simply experimenting, prompted by curiosity, or they

may have discovered that this method of providing fric-
tion is more pleasurable than self-stimulation. They may
not be at all attracted to each other in any sexual sense,
and such activity is hardly more "homosexual" than is masturbation itself.

Much male prostitution differs from sexual activity of
this kind only in the added inducement of payment. Other
examples could be given illustrating homosexual activity in
the absence of *attraction to the person.*

Homosexuality comparable to normal amorous behavior begins with personal attraction, and the emotion experienced is sexual even though it may never lead to physical
contacts. Thus, just as repeated sexual contacts with one of
the same sex may not be homosexual, a relationship quite
lacking in such contacts may be genuinely so. Many of the
latter are in fact "platonic" to the degree in which emotional attraction is much more important than physical intercourse of any kind.

Research has further revealed that sexuality is emphatically not an either-or matter: that all persons cannot, for
example, be classed as normal, homosexual, or bisexual.
There are a great many *intermediates* of variable degree,
the Kinsey investigation indicating that nearly half of a
large sampling of men had responded sexually to persons
of both sexes sometime in the course of their adult lives.
One of the results was a seven-point scale, with a person
who had never engaged in homosexual behavior or felt
such attraction rated at zero, while one whose contacts and
attractions had been limited entirely to his own sex would
be rated at six.

Sexuality thus becomes a matter of "ratios," and here
again inclination and behavior may differ. A person at or
near the midpoint in scale position, being fairly equally
attracted to both sexes, may in practice have had much
more contact with one sex than the other, owing to the

availability of partners or to fear of the social disapproval of homosexual behavior. Two persons of equal scale positions may thus have very different histories of sexual experience.

One reason for including discussion of same-sex attraction in this study is that personalized esthetic response and the arousal of amorous emotion may be fully as important a part of it as in normal sexual love. Here another "scale" might be worked out, but in this case showing the changing proportions of esthetic and sensual components, and ranging from attractions in which one predominates to those heavily weighted with the other.

Precisely as in normal sexuality, homosexual interest may be strongly physical, or body-centered, in some instances the word "beauty" itself having apparently little or no esthetic meaning, its effect being almost entirely erotic. There are those, on the other hand, whose love-thoughts are strongly romantic and idealistic, with marked emphasis on the esthetic charms of features, voice, mannerisms or *style* of personality. There is a sense, too, in which sexuality may be physical yet nongenital, as with the homosexual who testified: "I can take sex or leave it. I'm not really interested in anything but looking at my lover and in kissing, caressing and stroking. 'Love' to me means gazing and touching and being close." Again as with the heterosexual, the homosexual's goal is often a stable and permanent relationship, with little interest in philandering, "playing the field," or "one-night stands." Emotional fixations may also create familiar emotional problems when a relationship is insecure or felt to be so: anxiety, jealousy, and excessive possessiveness.

The romantic element in same-sex attractions is often stressed in the literature, though more often by early students than by the more recent. One of them writes: "It would be a great mistake to suppose that their attachments are necessarily . . . connected with sexual acts. On the contrary, as abundant evidence shows, they are often purely emotional . . ." (Carpenter, 1908, p. 26). Another confirms this: "There are cases in which the manifestations of the instinct [i.e. homosexuality] are confined to the psychic sphere . . . Platonic love may show itself solely in an exalted admiration for the person beloved. In other cases it is characterized by a desire to touch, to kiss, without any conscious intervention of the genital sense" (Féré, 1932, p. 144). The concept of attraction as a ratio between amorous and sensual components is sometimes emphasized: "Ideal love and the gratification of the grossest sensuality are . . . the two poles between which the amatory manifestations of male homosexuals oscillate. Many confine themselves to simple contacts, caresses . . . and embraces" (Bloch, 1914, p. 509). What would commonly be regarded as simple "tender affection" rather than erotic exchanges is often reported by observers in this field in an effort to correct erroneous notions about this deviation as a "degraded" variety of sexual indulgence. "With not a few homosexuals it may be a matter only of kissing and caressing and never of sexual activity in the narrowest sense of the word . . ." (Kahn, 1931, p. 136).

Examples are numerous, in the literature of homosexuality, of the separation of sensual from amorous attraction, some being clearly parallel to those reviewed earlier in the context of normal sexual love. Each of the following is from a different source.

> At the age of puberty he dreamed in two ways, but always about males. One species of vision was highly idealistic; a radiant and lovely young man's face with floating hair appeared to him on a background of dim shadows. The other was obscene, being generally the sight of a groom's or carter's genitals in a state of violent erection. (Ellis, 1936, I, 4:281)

Toward the end of this period of [promiscuous genital play] there was a new and increasing development of another sort, not recognized then as at all sexual in character. He began to feel toward certain boys in a way very different and much keener than he had done thus far toward girls, although at the time he made no comparisons. . . . Sexual matters were never discussed or thought of. These experiences were, in their way, very sentimental and ideal. [He] is sure that with himself the main consideration was always the other boy's beauty. (Ellis, 1936, I, 4:187–88)

I was fifteen years . . . old when the first erotic dream announced the arrival of puberty. I had no previous experience of sex satisfaction, either in the [homosexual] direction or in any other. . . . From a much earlier time, however, I had been subject partly to tender yearnings and partly to sensual longing without definite form and purpose—the two emotions being always separate from each other and never experienced for one and the same man. (Carpenter, 1908, p. 142)

[A boy of sixteen describes an amorous experience:] I would have died for him ten times over. My devices and plannings to meet him . . . were those of a lad for his sweetheart, and when I saw him my heart beat so violently that it caught my breath, and I could not speak. We met in —— and for the weeks that he stayed there I thought of nothing else . . . thought of him night and day . . . and when he returned to London I used to write him weekly letters, veritable love-letters of many sheets in length. . . . The passion, violent and extravagant as it was, I believe to have been perfectly free from sex-feeling and perfectly wholesome and good for me. (Carpenter, 1908, p. 84)

A remarkable episode in the sexual history of mankind was the wide currency and social acceptance of homosexual attraction among the classical Greeks. Had this been based on erotic interest alone there would have been nothing notable about "Greek love," since the more sensual variety of homosexuality has had a long history among Oriental nations. The "platonic" relationships of the Greeks is of importance here because of the evidence that it included to a highly distinctive degree the amorous component of attraction which is our central interest.

The boy-love of the ancient Greeks was unusual, according to a thorough student of the phenomena, in that it was to a high degree characterized by the same romantic attitude and emotion so often regarded as the unique feature of the more ideal form of attraction between man and woman. It closely resembled the kind of amorous romanticism associated with the age of the troubadours and the cult of woman worship in Western Europe during the Middle Ages. This emotion "is precisely the same in quality . . . whether the object which stirred it was a young man in Greece or a married woman as in medieval Europe . . ." (Symonds, 1901, p. 17). The boy-love described by Plato is closely similar to the inspiration and enthusiasm awakened in the knightly lover in contemplating the lady to whom he was pledged.

Many men of homosexual inclination seek virile and masculine qualities in other males and are repelled by any traits suggestive of the feminine. The military man as a symbol of masculinity may for this reason have been attractive among the Greeks, since valor and hardihood were highly prized. It has been suggested that the Greek form of homosexuality arose out of military comradeship when many men, on campaigns for long periods, far from home and from feminine contacts, grew close to each other. (Symonds, 1901). Similar attachments develop in prisons and other circumstances of isolation from the opposite sex, but in such instances the emphasis falls more on erotic needs and sensual gratification. The Greek type of homo-

sexual attraction differed from these in its strong emphasis
upon a masculine form of the romantic sentiment. Here it
may be said, simply, that the object differed but the emotion was the same.

Homosexuality and the Origins of Romantic Emotion

How does the romantic form of attraction develop; is it
acquired during the growth process, or does it have a
deeper source?

All signs, directives, and influences in every society
point toward the opposite sex. It would be easy to infer
from this that normal attraction is but one of many attitudes informally absorbed from the social environment.
As a later chapter will show, the history of the relationship
between men and women reflects in part the changes in
the esteem toward women in different ages and societies.

Equally plausible, however, is the thesis that the social
"tradition" of attraction between the sexes owes its origin
to a natural predisposition toward such attraction—that
culture reinforces biology. Changes in the character of
attraction from one epoch and locale to another are then
to be seen as no more than variations on a fundamental
theme; cultural influences may modify and color the
phenomenon, but they do not *create* it.

Which of the two possibilities is correct? Those who
have observed that boys do not need to be taught that
certain girls are "pretty" will favor the view that attraction
comes first, and that tradition merely follows it. Esthetic
responses of this kind have appeared to be as untaught as
response to the beauties of flowers, sunsets, and musical
melodies. Some theorists have argued that reproduction is
far too vital to Nature's purposes for sexual attraction to
be left to the uncertainties of the learning process.

Homosexuality offers some indirect evidence here, since

it would be surely paradoxical if normal attraction had to be learned while the deviant or "reversed" form of attraction is the expression—as many believe, and as much evidence suggests—of an inborn disposition.

The cases with which this chapter was introduced illustrate what many regard as impressive evidence of unlearned components of sexuality. The widely current view that homosexual behavior must be seen as a symptom of maladjustment in the normal direction is not easily reconciled with cases in which the heterosexual history leaves no question as to essential normality of the impulses, but where there is yet periodic or occasional strong attraction to persons of the same sex.

In reports on homosexuality among primitive people it has been noted that "no matter how a particular society may treat homosexuality, the behavior is very likely to occur in at least a few individuals." (Ford and Beach, 1951, p. 257). One survey of 76 primitive societies revealed that in two-thirds some form of homosexual behavior was regarded as "normal and socially acceptable for certain members of the community" (p. 130). Another investigator concluded a study with the statement that there "is probably no culture in which homosexuality has not been reported" (Taylor, 1965, p. 162). While all or most cultures thus have this in common, it is significant that social attitudes vary from rejection and ridicule to indifference or mere tolerance to acceptance and approval. In one group the deviant may be regarded as peculiar; in another, one who does *not* have such interests (along with normal impulses) may be classed as eccentric.

The occurrence of homosexuality in animals supports the view that it is universal behavior. "Frequent homosexual activity has been described for all species of mammals of which careful observations have been made. . . . It occurs in every type of animal that has been carefully studied" (Denniston, 1965, p. 38). In certain species "sexuality is extremely labile, with an individual functioning at times as a male and at other times as a female" (p. 42). Regarded as a significant parallel to human homosexual behavior is the fact that "homosexual arousal is much less frequent in females than in males" (p. 30)—this among female primates (subhuman) who at times exhibit male-like behavior.

Sexual mounting among the female of the lower mamals has been reported for domestic animals, for cattle, pigs, mice, and other forms. The male, in the absence of females, may approach other males, or a male may assume the usual sexual posture of a receptive female. A male may react normally to a female at one time and himself behave like a female at another. Females, also, may behave as males toward other females. This apparently *normal* behavior, from rats and rabbits to cattle and subhuman primates, suggests that the capacity for both male and female sexual responses is part of the heritage of vertebrate forms (Ford and Beach, 1951, p. 141).

These investigators regard it as "significant" that in the subhuman primates, as at the human level, homosexuality is more frequent in the male than in the female (p. 257). Biological rather than social factors seem to be indicated. Homosexual behavior is not, moreover, a substitute for normal sex activity in these animals, since it occurs when there is ample opportunity for normal sex activity. The behavior of the lower mammals indicates that the mating behavior of the individual organism is bisexual in the sense that the male nervous system is structured for female responses as well as for male, and that of the female is capable of male sexual behavior. The comparative evidence suggests that "a biological tendency for inversion of sexual behavior is inherent in most if not all mamals, including the human species" (p. 143).

Research on the origins of adult sexual behavior has placed great emphasis on the influences of childhood experiences within the family. A widely-held view of the sources of homosexuality centers on the process of the child's *identification* with one of the parents.

A family with an aggressive mother and a submissive father may be expected to affect the kind of personality a boy develops. If the mother is also the confidante and adviser he may lose respect for his father, will not want to be like him and will thus fail to develop a masculine point of view. The father may, on the other hand, be strict and punitive and frightening. In either case the grounds for identification will be lacking.

As a result of dominant maternal influence the boy may grow up with a weakness in masculinity; he will develop within the image of his mother. He will tend to lack aggressiveness and initiative. His shyness will be a handicap in approaching girls in the male role. His upbringing will better dispose him to adjust to them socially than sexually. His effemination and timidity will predispose him toward homosexuality by increasing the strains and challenges of becoming heterosexual.

A few studies have confirmed the importance of this formula in the family backgrounds of homosexuals. One investigator (West, 1957) selected, from the case histories of a group of deviates, certain characteristics of the parents relating to treatment of the children. These were compared with the same data from a group of nonhomosexuals. It was found that the homosexuals had markedly close emotional bonds with their mothers along with poor relationships with their fathers. The mothers tended to dominate the home, while for various reasons the father was a less effective personality.

Another researcher compared a hundred homosexuals with a hundred heterosexuals (Bieber, 1962). The mothers of the former were found to have had an excessively close bond with their sons; they were anxiously overprotective, interfered with the relationship between father and son, and failed to encourage a healthy attitude toward the opposite sex. The attitudes of the fathers of homosexual sons tended to be detached and hostile. By comparison with the heterosexual, the homosexual boy was much less often favored or accepted by the father. There were more conflicts; the fathers more often belittled and rejected the son, who tended to fear his father. These findings were taken to mean that male homosexuality results from family experiences which disturb or retard normal sexual development. It is assumed that normal impulses are always present but are inhibited by fear. The conclusion of this study and of similar ones is that all or most homosexuals are potentially normal but have failed to develop adequate masculinity through unfortunate parental influences.

Findings of this kind may be interpreted in a different way. The effeminate personalities of the boys who become homosexual may have *preceded* the maternal behavior as described above. The mother may have reacted as she did to the child because she found traits congenial to her own feminine personality, and the father may have found them uncongenial for the same reason. This view of the matter is permissible unless it could be shown that the children did not differ from birth in *any* of the traits which differentiate the sexes.

The negative cases in which the homosexual did *not* have an overclose bond with the mother, in which the father was not rejecting and rejected, and in which the son was not timid and did not tend to avoid masculine activity, are often overlooked. That the homosexual boy was the mother's favorite in two-thirds of the cases but not in all of them is a fact not to be by-passed. The mothers of homosexuals *encouraged* masculine behavior and attitudes in 17 percent of the cases and discouraged them in only 36 percent. In nearly every instance of a maternal attitude unfavorable to normal development there is a minority finding. This is clearly something to be considered, since homosexuality is itself a minority phenomenon.

The homosexual son felt accepted by his father in 23 percent of the cases. The father encouraged a masculine attitude in 45 percent. The son accepted and respected his father in 28 and in 20 percent of the cases.

The view that this deviation is a result of abnormal relationships between parent and child is widely held. The evidence suggests that such factors may have a part in the development of some cases, but certainly cannot be taken as showing that all are a reaction to fear of normal sexuality. Among other reasons there are too many instances in which the parental situations regarded as predisposing toward homosexuality are found in the developmental histories of quite normally sexed adults.*

* One investigator writes: "The simple fact is that dominating and seductive mothers; weak, hostile, or detached fathers . . . so often suggested as being etiologically significant in homosexuality abound in the histories of countless heterosexual individuals also, and cannot therefore be in themselves specific causative factors" (Marmor, 1965, p. 5).

The writer's own observations in a few intensive studies made in a clinical setting are well summarized in the statement that "Many male homosexuals assert that as far back as ever they can remember they have found their own sex attractive, but never have they had the least interest in women sexually (West, 1967, p. 181). The view that the esthetic-amorous component of attraction is an important and separable feature of homosexual attraction was clearly suggested long ago by one of the early students of this behavior: "If we turn to the close inspection of the detailed phenomena of this symptom complex, we see that in all cases of true homosexuality, long *before* the appearance of a homosexual act, the individual has felt strongly attracted, psychically, to certain persons of the same sex. This involuntary, pleasurably toned fixation of the senses and the mind occurs long before its sexual character, as such, enters consciousness." (Hirschfeld, 1914, pp. 42–43)

The Freudian theory of homosexuality, based on the premise that the male child's sexual love for his mother is in conflict with rivalrous hatred for his father—the famous Oedipus Complex—has been related to the development of romantic fixations. A parent, according to this doctrine, is the first person to arouse the sexual desire of the child. The parents being already possessed by each other, the child's desire at once encounters a rival, and this leads to fear and guilt. For the male child the fear is a response to the threat of castration, and both guilt and fear lead to repression of the desire.

Normally the conflict is outgrown as sexual attractions outside the family develop. In certain individuals, the theory holds, the emotional experiences of early life are unusually lasting in effect, and the Oedipus complex continues, creating anxiety and guilt in adult sex relationships. When the guilt and anxiety are strongly and firmly lodged, a normal adult relationship may be difficult or impossible because of transfer of the conflict to any attractive person. The female genital, instead of exciting the boy, arouses fear whose source is the childhood threat of castration. He may not be aware of the source of his anxiety owing to habitual repression of the conflict. There remains for him, as an erotic outlet, the members of his own sex, such attractions being free of conflict except so far as he may be affected by social disapproval of this kind of behavior. For the homosexual this must assumedly be the lesser evil compared with the still active childhood anxiety.*

* The doctrine that homosexuality arises from fear of the opposite sex may of course be considered apart from the Oedipus formula. Hostility and distrust may create similar conflicts. A youth who rejected his mother as completely as she rejected him irrationally spread his resentment to include the entire sex.

Those who see this deviation as a reaction to fear of the opposite sex often imply that it is to be regarded as a learned or "cultivated" substitute. It is therefore important to emphasize that in many instances it does not have this appearance, especially when the esthetic element in attraction is prominent. Emotion may be aroused, perhaps for the first time, by a particular individual. It is a sudden enthusiasm or appreciation—"sudden" in being immediate. The emphasis will be upon some characteristic of individual surface charm, as if a special response capacity had been awakened. The analogy of a musically gifted child responding to a new melody is suggestive; or, for that matter, of any person who is struck by a melodic phrasing which for him has a unique or unusual quality or appeal. The behavior and experience may, in brief, convey that some degree of homosexual responsiveness is inherent, with no more of learning than a normal boy needs instruction as to which of two girls is the prettier.

The evidence that certain kinds of parent-child relationships may be related to homosexuality is impressive. It is equally clear that the deviation may develop in their absence, and that it can fail to develop when they are present. Some males, unconfident about approaching the opposite sex, turn to their own as less threatening, but others with the same handicap do not do so. Some males, deprived of feminine association, as in prison, turn to their

---

In another instance there was fear of the mother, but fear of oppressive domination rather than of sexual attraction (or of castration) (West, 1967, pp. 146–50). One of my patients was fearful that marriage might threaten his freedom and initiative as his authoritarian mother ("She had a 'Hitler complex '") had blocked his spontaneity in nearly every direction. In another instance a youth's fear of "getting a girl in trouble" had been so deeply instilled that it rendered him unable to make any sexual approaches to women without anxiety.

own sex as a fair substitute, but others do not find this an acceptable solution. They do not have the choice because —as so much evidence suggests—they do not have the capacity to respond in this way.

The strength of the homòsexual preference in a culture so hostile to it as ours is often explained in terms of anxiety blocking normal sexual adjustment. However, as one writer has said, "it still remains to be demonstrated that such fears are *always* at the bottom of the homosexual symptom" (Marmor, 1965, p. 10). In certain cases where, despite copious evidence of successful performance in the heterosexual area, an individual finds himself struggling with a strong homosexual urge, anxiety is not a convincing explanation. The stress on anxiety as the determining motive *toward* homosexuality must seem paradoxical, moreover, to clinicians who have witnessed the panic into which a youth may be precipitated when he first becomes aware of homosexual impulses.

Concerning the aversion of some homosexuals to the female genitalia, the question has been asked: Where in nature can a group of males be found with such aversion to the genital organ of the female? Development of the esthetic sense beyond the level of the lower animals may provide a partial answer. Other parts of the female body may be specialized to attract esthetically, but the genitalia must first and foremost be structured for their function, with the consequence that they are, in this instance, esthetically unattractive. If we assume that some homosexuals are lacking in the desire that makes the female organ erotically exciting to the normal male, we may infer that its ugliness, esthetically viewed, might contribute to the aversion.

On the whole our findings suggest that esthetic attraction and amorous emotion are as important as aspect of same-sex relationships as of normal behavior; that many

such attractions clearly exhibit the same kind of spontaneity and immediacy often seen in the commoner variety of
romantic encounters; that in both forms the selective kind
of esthetic response to certain features ("fetishes") are
prominent. Such similarities strongly suggest that components of normal as well as same-sex attractions represent
unlearned forms of emotional responsiveness.

In summary we propose that the amorous-esthetic emotion is a basis for both homosexual and heterosexual attachments, and that the evidence for an unlearned factor
in same-sex fixations is one of several grounds for consid-
ering esthetic attraction between men and women as at
least as much a product of biology as of culture.

CHAPTER 8

The Sociology of Attraction

Psychological case histories and everyday observation show that family experiences greatly affect attitudes toward attraction and love choice. It is not so easy to demonstrate that the role of sexual attraction in life may be largely formed by subtle but powerful influences of the society into which each individual is born. Hitherto we have been concerned with the psychology and to some extent the biology of attraction and sexual choice; but at this point we must consider the effect of the culture in which the experience of attraction occurs—the sociology of sexual love.

The Social Setting

A book suggesting that romantic love as our age understands it is a new development in human history, unknown to the ancient world and to primitive peoples, was reviewed with skepticism by William James (1887). He could not believe that the powerful emotions aroused in attraction could be of recent origin. They must have had a longer history and deeper sources. What the historian of the sexual emotion had shown, he suggested, was not that a new feeling had appeared, but that a change had come about in the way this feeling was regarded, or *esteemed.* The issue was not its existence but its importance, its status as a life experience.*

Any age and society holds certain values and achievements in high regard as models or standards. One thinks of military virtues in ancient Sparta, of the drama or of athletic prowess in classical Athens, of artistic excellence in Renaissance Florence. At one time or place the most esteemed value may be commercial shrewdness (Carthage, Venice), or other-worldly piety (Mont St. Michel, Chartres); the religion of Rome, it has been said, was patriotism.

What a historian of the romantic experience could describe, (William James suggested), was not the birth of a new emotion but simply changes in *ways of thinking* about love. It would be a record of the ideas and attitudes about an emotion which was itself far older than any theories men might have about it. It would show that the way men think about their emotions does have an effect upon these experiences.

The point to be stressed is that the emotional effect of attraction will be much greater when its social status is high than when it is regarded as unimportant. There have been philosophies of attraction that gave it only a minor role in

* Suzanne Lilar (1965) is in an agreement with James, and includes herself among those "who do not consider love as a historical phenomenon or do not believe that at any stage men had to invent it, but hold on the contrary that it is one of the 'primitive data of the human condition' . . ." (p. 101). Similarly she rejects De Rougement's thesis that romantic love first arose in the twelfth century. Her own view, which she supports with impressive scholarship, is that the amorous emotion was in evidence in early antiquity; "already in Homer there are two kinds of love," the one romantic, the other companionate.

marriage and in human felicity generally. On the whole, it has been more often depreciated than exalted and its relative importance has been markedly lower than in contemporary America.

A number of factors affect the position any given society accords to amorous emotion. Among them, and perhaps as basic as any, is its "economic age." Amorous interest has been compared with artistic activity; it must wait for society to develop to the point at which leisure becomes possible. Romantic pursuits are a luxury not possible among a people who must focus all its energies on the exigencies of subsistence. Thus we find a relative lack of romantic sentiment among the more primitive cultures. A society must mature before it can release some of its members for what amounts to emotional recreation. "Capital . . . as a store of supplies relieving men from anxiety about maintenance, sets free the imagination to find attraction in the human form and so awakens sex emotion of a more refined order (Sumner and Keller, 1929, III:1509). In primitive or frontier societies, a woman's functions as a worker and breeder are far more important than any others. To her husband she was "slave, servant, property partner, plaything, child-bearer, long before she was friend or better self or soul-mate or affinity" (III:1520).

Social class differences are also important with regard to the setting favorable to romantic sentiment. However "civilized" a society, the difference between the leisured person at the top of the pyramid and the peasant or laborer at its base will affect the attitude toward sex. In eighteenth-century French society as described in Taine's *Ancient Regime,* for example, nobility and peasantry inhabit two entirely different worlds; the former's complete freedom from labor allowed them to dwell on things esthetic and amorous, while the latter had to concentrate on avoiding starvation.

East vs. West: Freedom of Choice

Other conditions have been equally basic. Freedom of choice is essential to the modern conception of romance and romantic marriage. The growth of sentiments of this kind are likely to be immediately checked when a society forbids or severely limits such choice. The practice of mate selection by parents has been widespread.

> In Japan, as in China and India, parents emphasize practical consideration—social status and economic standing—and ignore, on the whole, sentiment and personal preferences in arranging the marriages of their children. . . . Not alone in the Orient, but in ancient Greece and Rome and, indeed, among modern European peoples, marriage is still more a matter of family arrangement than of personal choice. . . . It is in the United States that perhaps the only, at any rate the most complete, demonstration of romantic love as the prologue and theme of marriage has been staged. . . . The relaxation of parental control over courtship has changed marriage into a romantic adventure. . . . The natural setting for romantic love is freedom of choice. (Burgess, 1926, pp. 290–94)

There have been many accounts of the contrasting attitudes toward romantic attraction held in Oriental and Occidental societies—the amorous response itself is essentially the same in both, but the social values have differed greatly. The West, in modern times, has glorified and idealized romance, while the East has tended strongly to scorn and reject it as a basis for marriage.

Two thorough students of the rationale and traditions of Eastern marriage have provided an excellent summary (Mace and Mace, 1959). They note, as have others, the wealth of literary evidence that the romantic experience has been well known in these cultures for thousands of years. In the two greatest epics of ancient India, for example, "stories of love are everywhere to be found." In the earlier ages in the Orient the amorous emotion flourished, but was progressively discouraged as a ground for marriage because it led to unwise choices and thus undermined the stability of the family. Attractions of this kind were also held to stimulate sexual license. Romantic love was finally outlawed because—paradoxically, from a Western point of view—marriage was regarded as too important to be based on so unreliable a foundation. While love themes persisted in poems and tales, the growing social disapproval during the Confucian era in China caused them to be given tragic endings.

In consequence of such a consensus Eastern marriages were typically arranged by the parents, who were assumed to be far better able to make a wise choice of matings. "It is a rigid principle of Eastern life that the stability of the family, and the maintenance of the social order, always come before the happiness of the individual. Romantic love is an unruly emotion, which out of control can do as much damage as uncontrolled anger" (p. 135). It is a saying among Asians, we are told, that "in the West you fall in love, then marry. In the East we marry, then fall in love."*

* This is a neat reversal of pattern, in theory, but its accuracy may be questioned when it implies that *romantic* love may develop as well after marriage as before in a parentally determined mating. If our thesis is true, and amorous emotion is aroused only in response to esthetic qualities, then post-marital romantic love could only occur when parental choices were based at least in part on traits in the esthetic category, and when they happened to coincide with the preferences of the person being mated in this way. Otherwise, while "love" might develop, it would be not the romantic sentiment but rather the kind of essentially sexless affection which usually does emerge in compatible marriages, independently of amorous feeling.

Another related aspect of the East-West contrast is the attitude toward any individualized interest between men and women, illustrated in the view that sex itself should be an impersonal relationship expressing a desire which may be satisfied by *any* member of the opposite sex. It was the *fixation* of attraction in romantic love which was regarded as a threat to domestic—and therefore to social—stability. Reflecting the clear difference between romantic attachment and conjugal affection, it was accepted that a man might fall romantically in love with one of that superior class of courtesans known as the *geisha,* while reserving a quite separate kind of feeling for his wife.* Even this indulgence, however, was regarded as a weakness. "Romantic feelings toward women in general were sternly discouraged." Nonetheless, the frequency of suicides resulting from frustrated amorous passion, especially in Japan, shows that the capacity for and urge toward such fixations cannot be suppressed.

Of course, recent rapid changes, owing to the effects of industrialization and to Western influence, have greatly altered the traditional Eastern attitudes in the direction of freedom of choice in marriage, greater independence and higher status of women, and the decline of patriarchal authority. These changes reduced the barriers to romanticism.

Effect of Status on the Romantic Attitude

An early investigator, certain that the esthetic response

* "In Japan particularly, the tradition has persisted that a man have two kinds of relationship with a woman—the dutiful but unexciting obligation he owes to his wife at home, and the less inhibited romantic experience he enjoys, in his free time and on a recreational basis, at the geisha house" (Mace and Mace, 1959, p. 129).

is basic to amorous emotion, emphasized that respect for the *person* must nevertheless be present, regardless of physical charm (Finck, 1887). One does not fall in love with a mental defective, for example, however beautiful. The *status* of women as a sex will therefore be of great importance. The very limited and much depreciated role of romantic love in Oriental marriage is in large part a reflection of the view of woman as biologically and psychologically inferior to man. Studies of Eastern marriage have made this clear. The subordinate position of women is linked with the patriarchal family. This male-and-father-dominated group has been vitally important in human social history. "The three great ancient civilizations that are the roots of Western culture—the Hebrews, the Greek, the Roman—were all completely patriarchal in their family life" (Mace and Mace, 1959, p. 51). Woman was primarily a household drudge and a breeder of children—always preferably of sons (daughters being a misfortune). She was regarded, moreover, as only a passive agent in reproduction, since the male seed was believed to be the true source of offspring; woman was merely the carrier, or the soil for the seed.

She was typically uneducated (a Brahmin proverb was: "Educate a woman and you put a knife in the hands of a monkey"), highly restricted in living pattern, mentally dull or unstimulating, and with little individuality. Obedience was seen as her chief virtue. A writer of the third century B.C. commented: "How sad it is to be a woman. Nothing on earth is held so cheap." She was expected to endure both neglect and abuse with patient resignation. "In China, in India, in Japan, it is the same story. The thought of the great Eastern cultures about the nature of woman shows little variation. And if that was what the East believed about her, we can only expect these ideas to be reflected in the way she was treated. (pp. 74–75). Even in cultures tracing descent through the female line women were regarded as inferior. The prevalence of the arranged marriage indicates how little a woman's preferences mattered.

The present high status of woman in Western societies is an historically recent development, in marked contrast with earlier centuries. "For every derogatory statement concerning women in the East, the West can produce a counterpart." The early founders of the Christian church are often cited for their severely degrading judgment of women as evil as well as inferior. Romantic love was associated with women of relatively high social status—for example, the women of the nobility during the age of chivalry and courtly love in medieval Europe. A woman regarded as an inferior may be sexually attractive, of course, but she is not likely to be an object of amorous emotion; she will not inspire *adoration,* which, one student stresses, "is absolutely essential to romantic love." In the medieval cult of romance and woman-worship the object of sentimental longing and devotion was usually of higher social position than that of her lover, the attraction of the loved one being inextricably linked with her *quality*—her aristocratic lineage or association with nobility.

A given society's definition of the woman's role will determine whether or not she will be viewed romantically. Her breeding function has often been primary, not only in primitive societies, but even in the most civilized culture of antiquity. "Nothing more profoundly distinguishes the Hellenic from the modern view of life than the estimate in which women were held . . . In ancient Greece, so far as our knowledge goes, there was little or no romance connected with the marriage tie. Marriage was a means of producing legitimate children . . . and we have no evidence that it was ever regarded as anything more (Dickinson, n.d., pp. 169–71). Apart from instances involving exceptional individuals, the Greeks were not romantic about women.

Emphasis on woman's *service* functions omits the essence of that which alone can give her meaning as a romantic companion: her individuality as a person. For antique and primitive societies she was a homemaker, a source of progeny and of sexual pleasure. Her use, rather than her self, was foremost in man's image of her. In Oriental civilization, to an even greater degree than in Greece, the attitude toward her was impersonal. Individual differences tended to be ironed out by the uniformities of social training and education. In traditional Oriental cultures, sexual love in its modern form, based on appreciation of the uniqueness of personality, did not exist. In this vein a student of marriage in China, states: "personal differentiation of feeling [and this refers mostly, if not entirely, to man] does not play a prominent part. Chinese lyrics do not sing of the one and only beloved, that lives once and will never be found a second time . . ." (Wilhelm, 1926, pp. 126–27). Regarding individuality: "Divorce was much more rare in ancient China than in modern Europe. There are several reasons for this, the main one being the great similarity of personalities, which do not express themselves according to individual taste, but according to strict social rules. Consequently it does not make much difference to a man which women he marries, for they are all more or less alike" (pp. 132–33).

In Europe, as the influence of Christianity grew, its emphasis on the importance of the individual aided the development of the new emotion. The growth of sexual love during the Middle Ages has been traced in part to awareness of the value of personality in the sex relationship. This stress on the role of the *person* is clearly related to our treatment of amorous emotion as based on choice, since choice is meaningless without awareness of individuality.

The new romantic emotion was really born when sex partners came to be seen and valued as unique individuals.

The value one assigns falling in love may be much affected, as we have said, by family experiences; it may also reflect the prevailing social attitudes toward personal attachments.

An example of particular interest because of its sharp contrast with our own culture is given in Margaret Mead's study (1928) of the Samoans. Here is a people whose philosophy of human relationships is markedly unlike ours, with corresponding effects on the attitude toward attraction. The emotional life of the Samoan is pitched at a much lower level of intensity. It is as if the exhortation to "take it easy" has become the keynote of an entire society. The typical Samoan is, by our standards, an unimpressionable person whose casual attitudes and shallow feelings might strike us as emotionally feeble. Samoa "is a place where no one plays for very high stakes, no one pays very heavy prices, no one suffers for his convictions or fights to the death for special ends . . . No one is hurried along in life or punished harshly for slowness of development. . . . From the first months of life . . . the lesson is learned of not caring for one person greatly, not setting high hopes on any one relationship" (p. 128).

Samoans have a "low level of appreciation of personality differences." Personal feelings and attachments are mild in degree. "Love and hate, jealousy and revenge, sorrow and bereavement, are all matters of weeks." Conflicts are few here, stressful situations are rare. Avoidance of deep feeling, or lack of it, has become "the very framework of all their attitudes toward life."

Owing in large part to these attitudes there is little appreciation of individuality and little tendency for personal feelings to become specialized. In a setting of this kind strong fixations do not occur. Attractions are lacking in intensity and tend to be transient. Romantic attachments are brief, by our standards; the natives were incredulous when told stories (e.g., Romeo and Juliet) about lasting devotion and fidelity. A frustrated love affair, in their thinking, should be easily replaceable by another. The bearing of all this upon amorous emotion is clear: "Romantic love as it occurs in our civilization, inextricably bound up with ideas of monogamy, exclusiveness, jealousy and an undeviating fidelity does not occur in Samoa" (Mead, 1939, p. 105).*

Historical Perspectives

It is our view that there have been some romantic attractions at all periods of human history (and prehistory) and in every society, regardless of the status of women or of the value set on their esthetic charms. The amorous life does have a history, however, in the sense that attitudes toward it have varied. As people have esteemed or depreciated it, its development has been advanced or retarded, and it has been more prominent in one time and place than in another.

If, as evolutionists tell us, human development has been cultural rather than physical for many thousands of years, and if man, psychologically, has been as he is now for an equal duration, the esthetic appreciation of sexual beauty is not a product of the historical epoch. Indirect evidence may be found in such data as we have on early human

* It is of interest that Mead observed individual differences in emotional temperament; not all were able to adjust easily to the conventional casualness. There were some with a capacity for emotion greater than that of their fellows. These were misfits, unable to take defeats lightly, or to change goals easily.

It should be noted, too, that so shallow a level of emotionality is not characteristic of all primitive societies, as Mead indicates.

artistic activity. The quality of certain prehistoric cave paintings suggests that man has been an artist for many millennia, and if he could then draw and paint impressively well, his appreciation of sexual beauty may have been as well developed. Concerning the animal drawings of the Altamira caves, roughly dated at about 16,000 B.C., an historian writes: "Conceivably they were just plain art, drawn with the pure joy of esthetic creation; the crudest representation should have sufficed the purpose of magic, whereas these paintings are often of such delicacy, power and skill as to suggest . . . that art, in this field at least, has not advanced much in the long course of human history" (Durant, 1954, pp. 96–97). If from such sensitive execution we may infer equally sensitive perception, it may be surmised that these people were not less appreciative of the opposite sex than of animals.

The legend of Helen of Troy centers on a woman who was very beautiful. If the spirit of romance was there, it was lost as the centuries passed, so far as the record goes. During the Homeric period there is no trace of the romantic attitude, according to a student of Greek poetry (Benecke, 1896). The classic tragedies include character studies of women, their passions and their "power for good or for evil," but they are not romantic figures. What little poetry was addressed to women was "entirely sensual" in content.

Apart from legends a fair case has been made for the beginnings of modern sexual love in the attractions of Greek men to the famous, or notorious, courtesans (*hetaerae*) of the classic period. These "noble companions," who combined beauty with refinement, culture, and wit, aroused emotions and led to behavior suggestive of more than sensual desire. It appears to have been, in some instances, the genuine romantic passion, but if the Greek male could fall in love with a courtesan, he rarely did so with the woman he married. Historians of social life and of marriage seem agreed that the Greek wife was essentially a breeder and housekeeper. The service functions of marriage were her total sphere; the companionate function was absent. She was unable to share in the intellectual interests of her mate.

Amorous Homosexuality in Greece

The widespread phenomenon of ancient Greek homosexuality has been interpreted as proving the bisexual potential of men anywhere, given a setting favorable to its expression. It has also been seen as evidence that the direction of sexual interest at any time or place is a *social* phenomenon; that is, something learned and transmitted. It must therefore be analogous to any other social movement, trend, or "contagion," since no one would seriously suggest that an entire society, or any large part of it, could be *biologically* abnormal.

The distinction between sensual and amorous behavior has been illustrated in earlier chapters. Homosexual attractions, as several observers have emphasized, may be relatively free of genital-sexual contacts and of desire for such contacts. The emphasis is prominent in a study of the "Greek phenomenon" which regards it as extraordinary not so much in its acceptance by a large part of this society as in its remarkably idealized character (Symonds, 1901). The *sensual* varieties of homoeroticism were well known to other ancient peoples. In classical Greece it was uniquely romantic, often to the exclusion of the sensual component of attraction.

Greek pederasty, or "boy love," was first of all a relationship between a youth and an older man. In almost every reference there is emphasis on esthetic admiration. While the ideal youth is amiable, modest, and intelligent, he is above all beautiful. "The adolescent boy, with his immature, half-girlish face and body, his unfolding mental powers, and his promise of ultimate manhood, could inspire the Greek man with an emotion still more intense and passionate than that aroused by the hetaera. Far from being a purely genital deviation, it involved refined, aesthetic moods startlingly like those more usually felt by a romantic man for a beautiful young girl" (Symonds, 1901, p. 7).

There is no novelty whatever, for a modern reader, in the words used in describing the emotion aroused by a handsome boy, nor is anything missing; the sole difference is the sex of the object. The obsessive preoccupation, the worshipful longing, the miseries of frustration and hopeless desire are all easily recognized. The identity of amorous pederasty with romantic heterosexual attraction seems beyond question.*

Arising in military comradeship among men separated for long periods from women, the attachments were linked with the masculine qualities developed in warfare. The term "boy love" is evidently inaccurate in this context, since the males must all have been old enough to bear arms. Some students have proposed that Greek homosexuality was truly bisexual in that an immature lad is in some

---

* Yet the earliest literary expression of this emotional state has been traced not to a male, but to the poetess Sappho of Lesbos (sixth century B.C.), the founder of "Lesbianism," whose amorous passion for young girls was the complete equivalent of the male adoration of boys: "most of the symptoms from which lovers have suffered for nearly twenty-five centuries were first set forth by Sappho. . . ." This was "something new, something not to be found in primitive life, poetry, or stories. This was the beginning of Western love. . . ." (Hunt, 1959, p. 44). Its beginning, then, was extramarital; Sappho, like the "homosexual" Greek male, had a spouse and a family, but wrote no romantic poetry about them.

respects intermediate, exhibiting girlish traits (voice, beardlessness) along with the beginnings of physical maleness. It has been suggested, however, that the effeminate homosexual would have found no place in classical Greece, where the relationship in its ideal form was masculine on both sides with no tolerance for softness of any kind. Yet evidence of both the military and the pederastic types of attachments is available, with no psychological grounds for excluding either. Here, the concept of bisexual *ratios* may be usefully applied.

We note again a familiar feature of sexual love: there were two levels of the masculine passion, a difference of which the Greeks were fully aware. There was a "higher" and a "lower" kind of attraction: "a noble and a base, a spiritual and a sensual"; the distinction is fully equivalent to the "two kinds of sex" of our earlier discussion. The sensual variety of boy love was not, of course, peculiar to Greece. "Vice of this kind does not vary to any great extent, whether one observes it in Athens or in Rome, in Florence of the 16th century or in Paris of the 19th . . ." (Symonds, 1901, p. 7) The love of an adult Greek for a youth, while not always free of sensuality, rarely became or remained an unalloyed physical liaison. It was often exalted as a truly ennobling emotion, in a way comparable to the "inspiration" often associated with modern romantic passion—as the kind of experience that brings out the best qualities, that heightens the self-esteem, raises morale and makes the lovers incapable of unworthy acts. "To be loved was honourable, for it implied being worthy . . . To love was glorious, since it pledged the lover to self sacrifice. . ." (p. 16). Greek love, like the modern romantic fixation, had dignity as a stimulus to nobility of character. "The effect produced upon the lover by the presence of his beloved was similar to that inspiration which the knight of romance received from his lady" (p. 8).

The latter parallel is striking, not only in the evidence of the identity of the amorous emotion in its antique and in its later (medieval) phases, but by its effect on the personalities of the lovers. In its highest form, Greek love was a spur to heroic endeavor. For the knight of chivalry, centuries later, the same emotion was a motive to bravery, courtesy, and adventurousness. Both relationships were independent of marriage, and in both there was a striving to keep sensuality in check. It may be incidental that in the background of both was a martial tradition.*

The Influence of Christianity

A study of *The Natural History of Love* (Hunt, 1959) provides many illustrations of the changing image of woman through the centuries as it affected her role and status as an object of attraction to man. Some features of the medieval period may be briefly outlined.

Following the Greeks of the "classic" age the amorous emotion went into decline. The Romans, practical and unimaginative realists, were not generally romantic about women. The Roman matron was a "respected subordinate," and her status improved markedly as her influence grew, but the sexual life, with the decline of the empire, became increasingly sensual and adulterous. This period

* "What is impressive about Greek homosexuality," writes Suzanne Lilar (1965), "is the quality of those who practiced it: certainly not the whole of Greece was homosexual—not by a long way—but incontestably its *elite* was" (p. 53). The classical Greek was homosexual, she suggests, in proportion as he desired to be regarded as heroic, manly and soldierly. There were men who fell "passionately" in love with women, but they did not boast of it, since it was regarded as unmasculine.

Many, on the other hand, disapproved of boy-love and ridiculed it. The Platonic doctrine of eros, with its origin in homosexual experience, was to become, nevertheless, highly influential, "the one and only great Western philosophy of love."

contributed little to the history of sexual love; but with the rise of Christianity, the image of woman changed for the worse.

In part as a reaction to the excesses of Roman society in its decadence, a strain of asceticism and antifeminism set in even before Christian morality had become widely current. Religious influence on the sex-emotional life was a development and an expansion rather than an entirely new chapter. Biblical sources were found to justify a growing negativism toward woman as a source of sin and shame. It was with St. Paul that her image as a symbol of Eve's guilt, of the Temptation, Original Sin and Fall was established. ". . . Christianity developed a fanatical fixation about the glory of virginity, the evilness of woman, the foulness of sexual connection, and the spiritual merit of denying the flesh and repudiating love" (Hunt, 1959, p. 104). Sexual love became suffused with guilt, a transgression against God. Formal indictments were made against woman, and much was written to link her with evil, to degrade her as a person, and to reduce her attraction as a sex.

Marriage itself was seen as a failure in Christian dedication. Even marital love became an emotion of doubtful value, and marital lovemaking a "temporary separation from the holy spirit." The result of all this, since natural desire and attraction could not be abolished, was a vast complex of ambivalence. The status of women was damaged legally as well as spiritually. She became more a piece of property, less an individual with rights and dignities. In such a setting amorous emotion in any romantic sense was hardly possible.

The Medieval "Romantic Movement"

How, in so unfavorable a soil, could the romantic sentiment and emotion develop? In its medieval form it was a truly new birth, and without clear historical origins. Its emotional quality and effects were anticipated in Greek pederasty. It was essentially an extramarital phenomenon. Adulterous relationships were common enough in Rome, but they were sensual rather than romantic. Christianity stressed the importance of a love free of "carnality" but certainly did not encourage the adoring attitude toward woman so prominent in the medieval cult of woman-worship.

Its origins have been traced in studies by Robert Briffault (1927). Romantic sentiment and sexual love, as now understood, first appeared in the popular literature, or "romances," of the French Middle Ages. These sentiments are distinctly European, in Briffault's view; nothing in any other culture is closely comparable. As expressed in the literature they refer exclusively to extramarital relationships. The great love stories "which for ages thrilled the imagination and stirred the emotion of European populations, in Saxon and Norman England as in Italy and Spain, are, without exception, from Tristan and Iseult, Lancelot and Guinevere, Eric and Enid, to Paolo and Francesca, presentments of illicit relations" (III:430).

Briffault finds some of the roots in the primitive societies of pre-Christian Europe. Narratives with themes of deep and passionate emotion, "obsessive and persistent," are found in ancient Celtic literature. This literature became Christianized over the centuries. In the conventions of later "courtly love" the emphasis on extramarital romance was linked with the pagan background, while the attempt to exalt it as something free of sensuality was a concession to Christianity, in the view of Briffault, "a . . . defense of the old usages and conceptions amid the new order and the new morality of Christianity."

The romantic sentiment may here be related to the status of women in pre-Christian Europe; they were "independent and influential." It may also reflect something in the emotional character of the Celtic temperament.

Most people—it should be safe to say—however little they may know of what love was like in bygone times, have learned that something romantic happened in the age of knighthood and chivalry: that there were troubadours, love-songs and highborn ladies whose love was a prize to be won by suitors who rated it worthy of great efforts. Such imagery might suggest a rather frivolous kind of amorous activity and there was indeed an apparent element of playfulness in some of its phases, but it turned out to be "a game that became a reality." What began as an amorous pastime finally became an important chapter in the history of the sex relationship. Any teen-age boy of this century who has become enamored of a girl, who spends much time thinking about her, whose thoughts of her are chaste, who writes a few verses to her or about her and engages in athletic feats with the hope of impressing her, would understand the feelings of the amorous, imaginative, and impressionable knights of the twelfth century who were the heroes of the new romantic movement.

"Noble" or courtly love was in many ways little more than an elaboration of such sentiment and maneuvers. The approach to the highly idealized love object was often gradual, indirect, and very patient. The restraint as well as the courtship might be heroic, and seemed at times like a deliberate effort to prolong the process until it became almost an end in itself. In contrast to the modern romance, the lady was usually married and the conventional finale therefore impossible. There was a sharp separation, however, between amorous emotion and sexual desire. The conviction was strong that through the exalted quality of this experience the character as a whole would be improved and elevated: "pure" love was itself purifying, and so had value for the ethics of behavior.

Many virtues of the adored lady were acknowledged in this cult, but none so much as beauty. The central place of esthetics in our treatment of the "love choice" is well illustrated here; beauty was even identified as an aspect of divinity.

Throughout these centuries the antisexual influence of the Church persisted. Woman's beauty was conceded but it was a sinister beauty, for its lure led to evil temptation and the lusts linked with damnation. The threat symbolized by her seductive attraction was not underplayed by an age that believed in witchcraft and was exhorted to see every feminine charm as a device of the devil.

Sexual beauty thus had two quite different meanings during this period. For the Christian it was dangerous enough to taint or destroy any impulse toward appreciation. For the devotee of the knightly cult the adoration of beauty in its ideal form helped man to glimpse one of the attributes of God himself. It was a difficult conflict to resolve. Love and sex continued to run in separate channels; the romanticist kept his ideal preoccupations in one compartment, his domestic interests in another. Dante and Petrarch were quite able to enjoy normal family lives while building their fantasies in an exotic private world. Marriage continued, as it had for centuries, to be arranged mainly by the families involved and to be concerned with income, property, and dowries.

A student of Greek literature has written of what he regards as the earliest expression of sexual love of man for woman as a modern would understand it (Benecke, 1896). This was a poem "entirely different from any love poem which had preceded it," in which such feelings were treated in a serious tone. It conveyed "the idea that a woman is a worthy object for a man's love, and that such love may well be the chief, if not the only, aim of a man's life."

The poem was much admired, and influenced other writers. It was written, however, not to a mistress or sweetheart, but to the wife of the poet, and after her death. It is probable that the sentiment was not so much of the romantic variety as of the deep emotional bond of affection that develops over a long period of close association. The study is important, however, as an illustration of the possibility of a change in the status, or value, of an emotion that may be brought about by an individual expression of experience.

There were other examples of individual centers of influence, each probably reflecting an unusually impressive experience. Among the better known and often cited is that of Ulrich von Lichtenstein, who spectacularly *lived* the themes of knight errantry and woman worship. William, Duke of Acquitaine, was the source of much amorous versification. Chretien de Troyes wrote of Lancelot and Guinevere and provided a popular model for many stories of knightly deeds in the service of adored ladies.

The truly modern period of the history of the amorous emotion began when the idea of romantic love was introduced into marriage. An historian of the theme finds literary evidence of this merger as early as the sixteenth century. Certain events and centers of influence were important. The love affair of Henry VIII and Anne Boleyn, for example, showed that a romance could have even greater power than political considerations. This famous episode advanced the view that marriage for love was worthy of respect. The "romantic idea," its modern origin in courtly circles, then began to work its way down into the middle classes, slowly becoming accepted as a normal preface to matrimony.

Some students of marriage doubt the usual assignment of the modern romantic sentiment to feudal society, since

the cult of that period typically involved extramarital relationships. A more favored view is that the more romantic
view of marriage—based on choice rather than family interests—may be traced to upper-class liaisons of seven-
teenth and eighteenth century France. The highly
cultured women of the salons, like the *hetaerae* and courtesans of antiquity, became the objects of true romantic sentiment, such attachments growing in esteem through the
quality of these women. Eventually their status was such
that the liaisons were often legitimized in marriage (Burgess, 1926).

A few of the factors that have shaped the evolution of
sexual love have been indicated: the economic development of a society, the status of women, the appreciation of
individuality, the influence of the Christian religion.
These factors have determined the value a society gave to
sexual attraction and the esteem in which it was held as a
motive. They affected the outcome of encounters between
the sexes; they created a sociology of attraction.

Individual responses must not be overlooked, however,
since all attitudes and values originate in and are expressed through them.* Often in accounts of a people
described as one in which marriage is a family arrange-
ment with woman as a property rather than as a person,
and in which, "consequently," there is little romance, we
come upon examples of exceptions—extraordinary attractions, sometimes leading to clashes with family pressures

* One may tend to forget, at times, that this is true of even
the broadest of institutional controls. Briffault (1927), writing of
the influence of medieval Christianity upon sexuality and the
image of woman, observes: "It is in the doctrines of Ambrose
and of Origen, of Augustine and of Jerome that European sexual morality has its roots" (III:506).

or with the mores of the group. Most such exceptional cases have no effects beyond the persons directly concerned, social customs being too powerful to be disturbed. But when the individual himself is also exceptional in some way, the beginning of a change is possible. With the literary gift he may have the influence of a Sappho, a Dante or a Petrarch (or a de Sade). The source may be a famous pair of lovers, real (Pericles and Aspasia, Abelard and Eloise), or fictional (Orpheus and Euridyce, Tristan and Iseult). Thus a combination of sex-emotional individuality, a vivid experience, or an exceptional personal influence of some kind has begun a reaction which radiates, patterned after the model, until a trend is under way.

Any history of a social evolution—of an art, for example—supplies examples. Aldous Huxley (1930), writing on "Fashions in Love," has suggested that while the basic source of the amorous emotion may be a constant, its history could be written, like that of art, in terms of periods, movements and styles. As an instance, he traces the upsurge of homosexuality in Europe following World War I partly to the writings of Marcel Proust and Andre Gide. Briffault (1927), in discussing the effect of religion on romanticism, writes: "the evolution . . . belongs . . . to the history of literature rather than to the history of life. Yet ultimately it is not possible to separate literature from life . . . the written page is the germ of the living mind of succeeding generations" (III:505).

Among the doctrines of modern romance is one of particular interest at this point: the belief, or faith, sometimes buttressed by certain feelings about personal destiny, that for each person there is an "affinity," or true mate, whose special qualities are the ideal complement for his own. This mate will thus provide the utmost of marital bliss. When encountered he will somehow be known, or recognized; there will be a feeling or a conviction that "this is he, or she."*

Whatever the origin of this article of faith, it appears to be now part of a popular folklore as to the meaning of attraction. Its *psychological* source has been indicated as one of the themes of this book: that the experience of attraction is most sudden and compelling when a particular encounter happens to correspond to the esthetic individualities of the persons concerned. It is likely that the doctrine of affinities was born out of some such experience of unusual impact. The likelihood of this origin would not depend greatly on frequency, since such encounters can be vividly impressive and memorable, as in some of the autobiographical accounts earlier illustrated.

While it is usually implied in discussions of sexual choice that attraction involves some degree of mutuality, it is notable that the emphasis nearly always falls on the image of woman as an object of attraction. There is little reference to changes in the attitude of woman toward man as a sexual partner. One historian of the relationship is quite definite on this point: woman has no sexual history because she has always been as she is now (Lucka, 1915). Never, for example, has there been a cult of adoration of the male comparable to that of the courtly romanticism of the Middle Ages.

The primary factor here is the response to physical beauty. Ford and Beach (1951) found it a "very interesting generalization . . . that in most societies the physical beauty

* G. R. Taylor (1953) traces back to Plato the modern idea of the "one and only true mate," in his theory that "every individual is but one half of a complete entity, so that somewhere there is to be found the twin-soul, the missing half . . . who provides the full complement for one's own personality." This is contrasted with an earlier view that "any two people, not obviously antipathetic, could probably make an effective marriage" (p. 197).

of the female receives more explicit consideration than does the handsomeness of the male," an observation confirmed by other students of sex behavior (p. 86). "Beauty in the human species is, above all, a feminine attribute, making its appeal to men . . . the normal woman experiences no corresponding cult for the beauty of man. The perfection of the body of man is not behind that of woman in beauty, but the study of it appeals only to the artist . . . it arouses sexual enthusiasm almost exclusively in the male sexual invert. . . . the man who is most successful with women is not the most handsome . . ." (Ellis, 1936, I,3:189).

Sex differences, however, are rarely exclusive; women have never been entirely indifferent to the esthetic values of men, though they have been trained not to express their admiration too graphically. Here again we are dealing, as with most psychological differences, with central tendencies rather than sharp divisions.

The Future of Amorous Emotion

The distinction between amorous and genital sexuality has been basic to this book. Prominent in much of the history of the relationship between man and woman, it was clearly drawn by the Greeks in their acceptance of sexual love as a vital part of emotional experience, to be treasured for its inspirational benefits. Christian doctrine distinguished between love and sex, and carried its rejection of the latter to the point of setting limits upon it even in marriage, an attitude which at times created ambivalent feelings about love itself. During the era of chivalric romance the two motives were widely separated, at least in theory, with sensuality seen as a contaminating alloy to be removed as far as possible from the ideal liaison.

Eventually the breach between amorous emotion and

sexual desire was closed, the modern ideal being a harmonious blending of motives upon the same person. A question remains as to the effect of increasing freedom of premarital sexual activity upon attraction and upon sexual love as a value. How will it affect the amorous emotion and the tradition of romantic marriage?

Part of the romantic tradition was that one can truly love but once, since only a person of "special design" could awaken the fullblown amorous passion. The individuality of the beloved gave a strong feeling of uniqueness to the experience, making it unthinkable that any other could inspire the same emotion—a thought repugnant in itself to the romantic mood. The sex act, when reserved for one person, completed the image of a distinctive bond, its intimacy making it a symbol of exclusive possession. Today, with increasing sexual mobility, the notion of the "one and only" affinity is breaking down. It is here suggested that neither amorous emotion nor the concept of romantic love will be lost with more extensive sexual freedom, but that some change in its quality may be expected as compared with that of the Victorian and early twentieth century periods. Obviously the relationship can no longer be unique in the traditional sense that an exclusive kind of physical belonging is an important part of it. The romantic experience in this sense must lose some of its individuality and therefore some of its depth.

Since the exercise of premarital freedom is a matter of degree, the issue it raises is not to be resolved in black and white terms. It is nonetheless true that since a person's sexual worth in the eyes of others depends in part upon the value he places on himself, his attractiveness will be diminished when that value is reduced by a large amount of "giving."

This is illustrated in the comments of an intelligent and very mature young woman on a person she was attracted to but had become seriously doubtful of marrying.

You are asking me to tell you how my knowledge of his sexual background affected my feeling for him, meaning the fact that he has been intimate with "several dozen" women (so he says). For one thing it would mean that he is not likely to be much impressed with my own "physical person," having been familiar with so many others. Since I've been rather highly selective in my own experiences it would make me feel a bit cheated that he would not appreciate me as much as I feel I deserve.

More important, however, is the way I feel about *him*. When I think of all those women it would be hard to have romantic thoughts about marrying him. I don't mean exactly that he is shopworn but that he has certainly been the opposite of hard to get. I can't think of him as having high standards of taste. It makes him a bit common somehow, and that would make a relationship with him a bit common too. I'm not trying to make any kind of magic out of sex. But I do think there ought to be *something* that sets one relationship apart from others if it really is different and if it is to lead to marriage.

Havelock Ellis, who gave much thought to the role of chastity in sexual love, regarded it as a vital part of what makes a woman romantically attractive. Without it, he believed, "It is impossible to maintain the dignity of sexual love." A promiscuous woman, as has often been said, may be sexually exciting but rarely inspires romantic sentiment. That there is a loss in attraction when sex is unrestricted is a view often encountered in the literature of sex psychology, usually expressed without further analysis. A great anthropologist once observed that almost all societies place some limits on sexual freedom, a restriction he attributes to a "realization" that sex must for some reason be *conserved:* "man seems everywhere and always to have felt that sex was a gratification that it was not well to secure at too easy a price . . ." (Sapir, 1930, p. 365).

With the perfection of methods of pregnancy control and the fact that commercial stimulation of the sex impulse is so profitable a business, it appears certain that sexual permissiveness will increase. In compensation for some loss of romantic quality there may be a gain when woman's role as a person and as a companion becomes more independent of her sexuality than has hitherto been true. As sex itself becomes less important simply because less inflated in value through repression and taboo, a shift may well come about in the direction of a higher esteem for woman's nonsexual assets—her personal qualities and interests, matters of character and personality that many women have wished to be prized for more than for their sexual assets.

A time may come when sex will be no more than an incidental and *relatively* unimportant staple of the love relationship, and when romance will be more nearly the emotional response to esthetic and personal individuality, without benefit of the physical frustrations which have long been regarded as essential to its flowering.

Sex Roles:
Nature vs. Nurture

A widely current view of sexual behavior is set in the reference frame of the social field in which it develops. It stresses cultural norms and modes as by far the most important
determinants. An example, somewhat extreme but clearly
illustrative, is that all differences between the sexes beyond
the anatomical are a product of social communication: of
upbringing and of attitudes assimilated from the larger
environment. This means, among other things, that the
perceptions and feelings of a boy, for example—his identification of himself *as* a boy as well as all his reactions to
girls—are ingrained (conditioned) by the setting into
which he is born. His sex role, sex interests, and motiva-
tions are socially molded outcomes. They will vary, moreover, as his culture varies—even within his lifetime—in the
character of its institutional or modal treatment of sex.

A reversed-sex example of the latter phenomenon
would be the great contrast between the norm for feminine behavior in the mid-nineteenth century and the norm
today—or still further, in the recent woman's liberation
movement. Early Victorian-American woman was a *haus-
frau* with narrowly limited interests and presumed capacities, sexually indifferent or at least utterly passive, with no

183

strong concerns beyond home, husband, and children. (Woodward, 1963, pp. 167–71). Contemporary woman— especially if actively liberationist in stance—has a completely different self-image with regard to sexuality, individuality, and economic status. The point to be stressed is that the concept of "femininity" has undergone and continues to exhibit rapid change in reaction to a variety of economic, political, and technological (e.g., birth control advances) transformations.

Sexual behavior in this view is essentially a culture product, socially created and no more than a variable reflection of whatever trends and role definitions happen to be current. "Masculine" and "feminine" are whatever the currently accepted images say they are, or should be.

This writer's first university major being in sociology, followed by thorough indoctrination in learning theory, my earliest orientation was—and *still is*—to search, always and everywhere, for the determinants of behavior among conditioning factors, subtle and pervasive social influences and culture traits. I still regard this as the first step toward the solution of any psychological problem.

Eventually and gradually, however, I found myself forced, during 21 years in a behavior clinic, in a psychiatric hospital, and in a practice in marital and premarital analysis and counseling, to modify some of my earlier views. My studies of emotional problems relating to sex roles, of the emotional relationships of the sexes in marriage, and of sex deviants, led to certain marked qualifications of my basic sociological orientation. I became convinced that while sex roles, for example, are *generally* a reflection of what society imposes, important allowance must be made for large individual differences in the reaction to culture norms. Some women, for example, react positively to the liberationist trend; it formulates their protests and offers answers and support for their needs. There are others, however, who are deeply contented with the traditional role and find it so fulfilling that they have difficulty in understanding those who reject it. Such differential reactions may be impressive and must be seen to have important meaning for sex psychology.

A further consideration concerns the *origin* of sex role norms, and here I can only say that I do not find references to "social-historical" sources adequate, or rather, I find them incomplete. How do they arise? One cannot extend the concept backward indefinitely without finally meeting the question of factors in the psychosexual make-up more basic than the transmission of cultural forms. Culture, as Maslow (1968) has said, "doesn't create a human being. It doesn't implant within him the ability to love, or to be curious, or to philosophize, or . . . to be creative. Rather it permits . . . or fosters, or encourages . . . what exists in embryo to become real and actual. The culture is sun and food and water; it is not the seed" (p. 161). Just as a biologist (Dobzhansky, 1966) can say: "Species and races are . . . derivative from individuals, not the other way around" (p. 46), so an anthropologist (Keith, 1947) observes: "Tradition is molded to fit the mentality which fashions it, not the other way round" (p. 48).

No one questions that children must learn the "facts of life" and other related facts of sexual behavior and practice, but there is little evidence that esthetic attraction is learned or that the difference in sex-esthetic response between males and females needs to be taught. Culture norms of what is beautiful do exist, but the pervasive individuality in response to these norms is further evidence, I suggest, of deeper sources of sexual behavior; that is to say, it appears that Nature did not entirely abandon this enormously vital sector of life after differentiating sexual anatomies.

References

Chapter 1—Introduction

Arnold, M. B. *Emotion and Personality: Psychological Aspects.* New York: Columbia University Press, 1960.

Binet, Alfred. "Le Fetichisme dans l'Amour." *Revue Philosophique* 24, (1887): 143–67, 252–74.

Blau, T. H. "The Love Effect." In *Love Today: A New Exploration*, edited by H. A. Otto, pp. 151–64. New York: Association Press, 1972.

Burton, Robert. *The Anatomy of Melancholy.* III. Boston: William Veazie, 1859.

Cameron, Norman. *Personality Development and Psychopathology.* Boston: Houghton Mifflin, 1963.

Finck, Henry T. *Romantic Love and Personal Beauty.* London: Macmillan, 1887.

Freud, Sigmund, *Group Psychology and Analysis of the Ego.* London: International Psychoanalytic Press, 1922.

Fromm, Eric. *The Art of Loving.* New York: Harper & Row, 1963.

Lilar, Suzanne. *Aspects of Love in Western Society.* New York: McGraw-Hill, 1965.

May, Rollo. *Love and Will.* New York: Norton, 1969.

Menninger, Karl. *The Vital Balance.* New York: Viking, 1963.

Moll, Albert. *The Sexual Life of the Child.* New York: Macmillan, 1924.

Reik, Theodor. *A Psychologist Looks at Love.* New York: Rinehart, 1944.

Sadler, W. A. *Existence and Love: A New Approach in Existential Phenomenology.* New York: Scribner's, 1969.

Walster, Elaine. "Passionate Love." In *Theories of Attraction and Love,* edited by B. I. Murstein, pp. 85–99. New York: Springer, 1971.

Chapter 2—The Amorous Emotion

Allport, Gordon. *Personality: A Psychological Interpretation.* New York: Holt, 1937.

Bell, Sanford. "A Preliminary Study of the Emotion of Love between the Sexes. *American Journal of Psychology* 13, (1902): 325–54.

Burgess, E. W., and Locke, H. J. *The Family: From Institution to Companionship.* New York: American Book, 1945.

Ellis, Havelock. *Studies in the Psychology of Sex.* I. New York: Random House, 1936.

———. *The Psychology of Sex: A Manual for Students.* New York: Emerson, 1946.

Freud, Sigmund. *Basic Writings of Sigmund Freud.* New York: Modern Library, 1938.

———. *Group Psychology and the Analysis of the Ego.* London: International Psycho-analytic Press, 1922.

———. *Collected Papers.* London: The Hogarth Press and The Institute for Psycho-analysis, 1933.

Grant, Vernon. *The Psychology of Sexual Emotion.* New York: Longmans, Green, 1957.

Hobhouse, L. T.; Wheeler, G. C.; and Ginsburg, M. *The Material Culture and Social Institutions of the Simpler Peoples.* London: Chapman & Hall, 1930.

Huxley, Aldous. *Do What You Will.* New York: Doubleday, 1930.

Huxley, Julian S. *Man Stands Alone,* New York: Harper, 1927.

Kinsey, A. C.; Pomeroy, W. B.; and Martin, C. E. *Sexual Behavior of the Human Male.* Philadelphia: W. B. Saunders, 1948.

Linton, Ralph. *The Study of Man*. New York: Appleton-Century-Crofts, 1936.

Lowie, R. H. *The Crow Indians*. New York: Farrar and Rinehart, 1935.

Malinowski, Bronislaw. *The Sexual Life of Savages in Northwestern Melanesia*. New York: Harcourt, Brace, 1929.

Mead, Margaret. *Growing Up In New Guinea*. New York: Morrow, 1930.

Reik, Theodor. *A Psychologist Looks at Love*. New York: Rinehart, 1944.

Sapir, Edward. "The Discipline of Sex." *The World Today* 55, (1930).

Sumner, W. G., and Keller, A. G. *The Science of Society*. III. New Haven: Yale University Press, 1929.

Symonds, Percival M. *The Dynamics of Human Adjustment*. New York: Appleton-Century, 1946.

Young, P. T. *Emotion in Man and Animal*. New York: Wiley, 1943.

Chapter 3—The Growth and Expression of Amorous Emotion

Bell, Stanford. "A Preliminary Study of the Emotion of Love between the Sexes." *American Journal of Psychology* 13, (1902): 325–54.

Binet, Alfred. "Le Fetichisme dans l'Amour." *Revue Philosophique* 24, (1887): 260.

Bühler, Charlotte. "Zum Probleme der sexuellen Entwicklung." *Z. Kinderheilk* 51, (1931): 612–642.

Eastman, Max. *Enjoyment of Living*. New York: Harper, 1948.

Ellis, Havelock. *Studies in the Psychology of Sex*. I. New York: Random House, 1936.

———. *My Life: The Autobiography of Havelock Ellis*. Boston: Houghton-Mifflin, 1939.

Freud, Sigmund. *Group Psychology and the Analysis of the Ego*. London: International Psychoanalytic Press, 1922.

———. *Basic Writings of Sigmund Freud*. New York: Modern Library, 1938.

Gesell, A., and Ilg, F. *The Child from Five to Ten*. New York: Harper, 1946.

Grant, Vernon W. *The Psychology of Sexual Emotion*. New York: Longmans, Green, 1957.

Hamilton, G. V. *A Research in Marriage*. New York: Albert and Charles Boni, 1929.

Jersild, Arthur T. *Child Psychology*. 6th ed. Englewood Cliffs, N.J.: Prentice-Hall, 1968.

Krafft-Ebing, R. V. *Psychopathia Sexualis*. Trans., 10th German ed. New York: Samuel Login, 1908.

Loewenfeld, L. *Uber die sexuelle Konstitution und andere Sexualprobleme*. Wiesbaden: J. F. Bergmann, 1911.

Moll, Albert. *The Sexual Life of the Child*. New York: Macmillan, 1924.

Moore, T. *The Works of Lord Byron with His Letters and Journals and His Life*. I. London: 1832.

Sears, Robert R. *A Survey of Objective Studies of Psychoanalytic Concepts*. Social Science Research Council Bulletin No. 57, New York, 1943.

Chapter 4—Individuality in Attraction: The Bases of Choice

Bell, Sanford. "A Preliminary Study of the Emotion of Love between the Sexes." *American Journal of Psychology* 13, (1902): 325–54.

Darwin, Charles. *The Descent of Man*. New York: A. L. Burt, 1874.

Ellis, Havelock. *Studies in the Psychology of Sex*. I. New York: Random House, 1936.

Folsom, Joseph K. *The Family and Democratic Society*. New York: Wiley, 1934.

Ford, C. S., and Beach, F. A. *Patterns of Sexual Behavior*. New York: Harper, 1951.

Langer, Suzanne. *Philosophy in a New Key*. New York: New American Library, 1948.

Lorenz, Konrad. *King Solomon's Ring*. New York: Time, Inc., 1962.

————. *On Aggression.* New York: Harcourt, Brace and World, 1963.

Lucka, Emil. *Eros: The Development of the Sex Relation through the Ages.* New York: Putnam's, 1915.

Reik, Theodor. *Listening with the Third Ear.* New York: Pyramid Books, 1964.

Santayana, George. *The Sense of Beauty.* New York: Scribner's, 1896.

Sullivan, J. W. N. *Beethoven.* Jonathan Cape, 1937.

Ward, Lester. *Pure Sociology.* New York: Macmillan, 1903.

Westermarck, Edward. *The History of Human Marriage.* 5th ed. I. London: Macmillan, 1925, p. 456.

Chapter 5—The Varieties of Esthetic Attraction

Berscheid, E., and Walster, E. H. *Interpersonal Attraction.* Reading, Mass.: Addison-Wesley, 1969.

Beyle, Marie Henri [Stendhal]. *On Love.* New York: Boni and Liveright, 1927.

Binet, Alfred. "Le Fetichisme dans l'Amour." *Revue Philosophique* 24, (1887): 143–67, 252–74.

Burton, Richard. *The Anatomy of Melancholy.* III. Boston: William Veazie, 1859.

Elder, G. H., Jr. "Appearance and Education in Marriage Mobility." *American Sociological Review* 34, (1969): 519–33.

Ellis, Albert. "A Study of the Love Emotions of American College Girls." *International Journal of Sexology* (August 1949) p. 4.

Ellis, Havelock. *Studies in the Psychology of Sex.* I. New York: Random House, 1936.

Elwin, Verrier. *The Baiga.* London: John Murray, 1939.

Grant, Vernon W. *The Psychology of Sexual Emotion.* New York: Longmans, Green, 1957.

Hall, Granville S. *Adolescence.* II. New York: Appleton-Century-Crofts, 1904.

Hamilton, G. V. *A Research in Marriage.* New York: Albert & Charles Boni, 1929.

Henry, G. G. *Sex Variants.* I. New York: Paul B. Hoeber, 1941, p. 250.

Hirschfeld, Magnus. *Sex in Human Relationships.* London: John Lane, 1935.

———. *Sexual Pathology.* Newark: Julian Press, 1932.

James, William. *The Varieties of Religious Experience.* New Hyde Park, N.Y.: University Books, 1963, p. 382.

Kahn, Eugen. *Psychopathic Personalities.* New Haven: Yale University Press, 1931.

Krafft-Ebing, R. V. *Psychopathia Sexualis.* Trans. 10th German ed. New York: Samuel Login, 1908.

Macaulay, Thomas B. *The History of England from the Accession of James II.* II. New York: Allison, n.d.

Malamud, Bernard. "The Magic Barrel." *A Malamud Reader.* New York: Farrar, Straus & Giroux, 1967.

Mann, Thomas. "Death in Venice." *Stories of Three Decades.* New York: Knopf, 1936.

Moll, Albert. *Untersuchungen über die Libido Sexualis.* Berlin: Kornfeld, 1898.

Nabokov, Vladimir. *Lolita.* New York: Putnam's, 1966.

Richardson, Henry H. *Maurice Guest.* New York: Norton, 1930.

Stekel, Wilheim. *Frigidity in Woman.* New York: Boni and Liveright, 1927.

Sumner, William G. *Folkways.* Boston: Ginn, 1906.

Chapter 6—The Role of Esthetic Attraction in Mate Selection

Bossard, J. H. S. *Marriage and the Child.* Philadelphia: University of Pennsylvania Press, 1940.

Burgess, E. W., and Wallin, P. "Homogamy in Personality Characteristics." *Journal of Abnormal and Social Psychology* 39, (1944): 475–81.

———. "Homogamy in Social Characteristics." *American Journal of Sociology* 49, (1943).

Burgess, E. W., and Locke, H. J. *The Family from Institution to Companionship*. New York: American Book, 1960.

Burgess, E. W., and Cottrell, L. S. *Predicting Success or Failure in Marriage*. Englewood Cliffs, N.J.: Prentice-Hall, 1939.

Davis, M. R., and Reeves, R. J. "Propinquity of Residence before Marriage." *American Journal of Sociology* 44, (1939): 510–17.

Goffman, Erving. "On Cooling the Mark Out: Some Aspects of Adaptation to Failure." *Psychiatry* 15, (1952): 451–63.

Hamilton, G. V. *A Research in Marriage*. New York: Albert & Charles Boni, 1929.

Huxley, Aldous. *Do What You Will*. New York: Doubleday, 1930.

James, William. Review of H. T. Finck, *Romantic Love and Personal Beauty*. In *The Nation* 45, (1887): 237–38.

Kephart, W. M. "Some Correlates of Romantic Love." *Journal of Marriage and the Family* 29, (1967): 470–74.

Kirkpatrick, Clifford. "A Statistical Investigation of the Psychoanalytic Theory of Mate Selection." *Journal of Abnormal and Social Psychology* 32, (1937): 427–30.

Lantz, H. R., and Snyder, E. C. *Marriage: An Examination of the Man-Woman Relationship*. New York: John Wiley & Sons, 1962.

Murdoch, G. P. *Social Structure*. New York: Macmillan, 1949.

Murstein, Bernard I. "A Theory of Marital Choice." In *Theories of Attraction and Love*, edited by B. I. Murstein, pp. 100–51. New York: Springer, 1971.

Nimkoff, M. F. *Marriage and the Family*. Boston: Houghton-Mifflin, 1947.

Reiss, Ira L. "Toward a Sociology of the Heterosexual Love Relationship." *Marriage and Family Living* 22, (1960): 139–45.

Strauss, Anselm. "The Ideal and the Chosen Mate." *American Journal of Sociology* 52, (1946): 204–8.

Terman, Louis M. *Psychological Factors in Marital Happiness*. New York: McGraw-Hill, 1938.

Walster, Elaine. "Passionate Love." In *Theories of Attraction and Love*, edited by B. I. Murstein, pp. 85–99. New York: Springer, 1971.

Walster, Elaine; Aronson, V.; Abrahams, D.; and Rottman, L. "Importance of Physical Attractiveness in Dating Behavior." *Journal of Personality and Social Psychology* 4, (1966): 508–16.

Winch, R. F. *Mate-Selection*. New York: Harper, 1958.

————. "Another Look at the Theory of Complementary Needs in Mate-Selection." *Journal of Marriage and the Family* 29, (1967): 756–62.

Chapter 7—Sexual Love: Instinct or Cultural Learning?

Adler, Alfred. *Social Interest: A Challenge to Mankind*. New York: Putnam's, 1938.

Benjamin, Harry. *The Transsexual Phenomenon*. New York: Julian Press, 1966.

Bieber, Irving. *Homosexuality: A Psychoanalytic Study*. New York: Basic Books, 1962.

Bloch, Ivan. *The Sexual Life of Our Time*. London: William Heinemann, 1914.

Breasted, James H. *The Dawn of Conscience*. New York: Scribner's, 1933, 1961.

Briffault, Robert. *The Mothers: A Study of the Origins of Sentiments and Institutions*. New York: Macmillan, 1927.

————. "Sexual Customs and Social Practice." In *The Making of Man,* edited by V. F. Calverton. New York: Random House (The Modern Library), 1931.

Carpenter, Edward. *The Intermediate Sex*. London: George Allen & Unwin, 1908.

Denniston, R. H. "Ambisexuality in Animals." In *Sexual Inversion,* edited by J. Marmor. New York: Basic Books, 1965.

Ellis, Havelock. *Studies in the Psychology of Sex*. I. New York: Random House, 1936.

Féré, C. *Sexual Degeneration in Mankind and in Animals*. New York: Anthropological Press, 1932.

Ford, C. S., and Beach, F. A. *Patterns of Sexual Behavior*. New York: Harper, 1951.

Hirschfeld, Magnus. *Die Homosexualität des Mannes und des Weibes*. Berlin: Louis Marcus, 1914.

Kahn, Eugen. *Psychopathic Personalities*. New Haven: Yale University Press, 1931.

Kinsey, A. C.; Pomeroy, W. B.; Martin, C. E.; and Gebhard, P.H. *Sexual Behavior in the Human Female*. Philadelphia: W. B. Saunders, 1953.

LaGache, D. "L'Amour et la Haine." In *Nouveau Traite de Psychologie*, VI, edited by G. Dumas, p. 130. Paris: Librairie Felix Alcan, 1939.

Lucka, Emil. *Eros: The Development of the Sex Relation through the Ages*. New York: Putnam's, 1915.

Lund, F. H. *Emotions of Men*. New York: McGraw-Hill, 1930.

Marmor, Juod, ed. *Sexual Inversion*. New York: Basic Books, 1965.

McDougall, William. *Outline of Abnormal Psychology*. New York: Scribner's, 1926.

Money, John. "Hermaphroditism." In *Encyclopedia of Sexual Behavior*, edited by A. Ellis and A. Abarbanel, pp. 472–84. New York: Hawthorn Books, 1961.

Montagu, Ashley. *The Natural Superiority of Women*. New York: Macmillan, 1968.

Symonds, John A. *A Problem in Greek Ethics, being an Inquiry into the Phenomenon of Sexual Inversion*. London, 1901.

Taylor, G. R. "Historical and Mythological Aspects of Homosexuality." In *Sexual Inversion*, edited by J. Marmor. New York: Basic Books, 1965.

Walter, E.; Aronson, V.; Abrahams, D.; and Rottman, L. "Importance of Physical Attractiveness in Dating Behavior." *Journal of Personality and Social Psychology* 4, (1966): 508–16.

West, D. J. *Homosexuality*. Chicago: Aldine, 1967.

Chapter 8—The Sociology of Attraction

Benecke, E. F. M. *Antimachus of Colophon and the Position of Women in Greek Poetry*. London: Swan Sonnenschein, 1896.

Briffault, Robert. *The Mothers: A Study of the Origins of Sentiments and Institutions.* New York: Macmillan, 1927.

Burgess, Ernest W. "The Romantic Impulse and Family Disorganization." *Survey* 57, (1926): 290–94.

Dickinson, G. L. *The Greek View of Life.* 7th ed. New York: Doubleday, Doran, n. d.

Durant, Will. *Our Oriental Heritage.* New York: Simon & Schuster, 1954.

Ellis, Havelock. *Studies in the Psychology of Sex.* I. New York: Random House, 1936.

Finck, Henry T. *Romantic Love and Personal Beauty.* London: Macmillan, 1887.

Ford, C. S., and Beach, F. A. *Patterns of Sexual Behavior.* New York: Harper, 1951.

Hunt, M. M. *The Natural History of Love.* New York: Knopf, 1959.

Huxley, Aldous. *Do What You Will.* New York: Doubleday, 1930.

James William. Review of H. T. Finck, *Romantic Love and Personal Beauty.* In *The Nation* 45, (1887): 237–38.

Lilar, Suzanne. *Aspects of Love in Western Society.* New York: McGraw-Hill, 1965.

Lucka, Emil. *Eros: The Development of the Sex Relation through the Ages.* New York: Putnam's, 1915.

Mace, D., and Mace, V. *Marriage: East and West.* New York: Doubleday (Dolphin Books), 1959, 1960.

Mead, Margaret. *Coming of Age in Samoa.* New York: Morrow, 1928.

———. *From the South Seas.* New York: Morrow, 1939.

Sapir, Edward. "The Discipline of Sex." *The World Today* 55, (1930).

Sumner, W. G., and Keller, A. G. *The Science of Society.* III. New Haven: Yale University Press, 1929.

Symonds, John A. *A Problem In Greek Ethics, being an Inquiry into the Phenomenon of Sexual Inversion.* London, 1901.

Taylor, G. R. *Sex in History.* London: Thames & Hudson, 1953.

Wilheim, R. "The Chinese Conception of Marriage." In *The Book of Marriage,* edited by E. Keyserling. New York: Harcourt, Brace, 1926.

196 *Falling in Love*

Epilogue—Sex Roles: Nature vs. Nurture

Dobzhansky, Theodosius. "Of Flies and Men." *American Psychologist* 21, (1966): 46–50.

Keith, Arthur. *Evolution and Ethics.* New York: G. P. Putnam's Sons, 1947.

Maslow, Abraham. *Toward a Psychology of Becoming.* Princeton, N.J.: D. Van Nostrand Co., 1968.

Woodward, William E. *The Way Our People Lived: An Intimate American History.* New York: Liveright, 1963.

Index

FE